HOW WE GOT OUR BIBLE

HOW WE GOT OUR BIBLE

T. C. SMITH

Smyth & Helwys Publishing, Inc.
Macon, Georgia

ISBN 1-880837-97-8

How We Got Our Bible
T. C. Smith
First Printing, April 1994
Second Printing, March 1995

Copyright © 1994
Smyth & Helwys Publishing, Inc.
6316 Peake Road
Macon, Georgia 31210-3960
1-800-568-1248

Printed in the United States of America.

The paper used in this publication meets the minimum
requirements of American Standard for Information
Sciences—Permanence of paper for Printed Library Materials,
ANSI Z39.48–1984.

Library of Congress Cataloging-in-Publication Data

Smith, T. C. (Taylor Clarence), 1915–
    How we got our Bible/T. C. Smith
    viii + 94 pp.   6" x 9" (15 x 23 cm.)
    Includes bibliographical references.
    ISBN 1-880837-97-8 (alk. paper)
    1. Bible—Canon   I. Title.
BS465.S53   1994   220.1'2—dc20

Contents

Contents

Preface

In talking with lay persons in churches, I have discovered that some are amazed to learn that there are questions about some of the books in the Bible. The answers that I seek to give should in no way be considered a devaluation of the Bible. When asked a question concerning the authority by which we accept all books in the Bible, the general response is, "That's the way it has always been." Even many students who are graduates of theological seminaries are not aware of the way our Bible has been transmitted to us. My hope is that this book will create sufficient curiosity for Christians to explore the history of the canonization of the Bible.

When Kurt Aland delivered a lecture before the Second International Congress on New Testament Studies that met at Christ Church, Oxford, in September 1961, he initiated a renewed interest of study in both the Old and New Testament canons. The subject of this lecture was "The Problem of the New Testament Canon." I was present for the delivery of the lecture and was inspired to continue my research in this area of study. In 1951 I had introduced a course on the New Testament canon at the Southern Baptist Theological Seminary, Louisville, Kentucky. The students were so much interested in the subject that it was my wish to include it in my courses until my departure from the seminary in 1958.

In 1964 I conducted a seminar at the Graduate Theological Union, Berkeley, California, on the "Canon and Text of the New Testament." The response of the students was most gratifying. The interest in the subject was so intense that I decided to write a book on how we got our Bible. In 1969 my presidential address before the Association of Baptist Professors of Religion was "A Reconsideration of the Canon of the New Testament." The address met with acceptance by the professors, but it was bitterly opposed by the fundamentalist news media.

After coming to the Religion department of Furman University, Greenville, South Carolina, I resumed my research and teaching on the canon. In retirement I have lectured on how we got our Bible at Southeastern Baptist Theological Seminary, Wake Forest, North Carolina; First Baptist Church and Berea Baptist Church, Mooresville, North Carolina; Christ Episcopal Church, Greenville, South Carolina; and Calder Baptist Church, Beaumont, Texas. In the spring of 1993 I was invited to give the

Coble-Morton Lectures at Northgate Baptist Church, Kansas City, Missouri. A portion of this book is the content of those lectures.

I am indebted to Ellen, my wife; Dr. Heber Peacock, United Bible Societies; Dr. Francis W. Bonner; Mrs. Doris Clanton; Mrs. Ann Quattlebaum; and Mr. Jack Dennis who read my manuscript and offered valuable suggestions.

                                                    T. C. Smith
                                                    Simpsonville SC
                                                    1 December 1993

Introduction

When Sir Walter Scott lay dying, he said to Lockhart, his son-in-law, "Bring me the book." "What book?" asked Lockhart. "*The* Book," replied Sir Walter, "the Bible, there is but one." We are emotionally moved by the reverence of Scott in regarding the Bible as *the* Book, but his declaration demands a clarification and a qualification. Which Bible is *the* Book? Is it the Jewish Bible, the Roman Catholic Bible, the Protestant Bible, the Ethiopic Bible, or the Orthodox Bible?

Since Jews and Christians rely upon the Bible for their understanding of faith and practice, they should know, without any doubt, what the contents of the Bible are. The Jews frequently refer to their Bible as Tanak; it includes the thirty-nine books of the Old Testament accepted by Christians. In the Bible of the Ethiopic Church there are additional books for both the Old and New Testaments—forty-six books for the Old Testament and thirty-five for the New, making a total of eighty-one. Roman Catholics have the same number of books in the New Testament as do Protestants, but for the Old Testament they have all the books of the Apocrypha except 1 and 2 Esdras and the Prayer of Manasseh.[1] Protestant churches generally consider the thirty-nine books of the Old Testament and twenty-seven books of the New as their Bible. Thus it is essential at the outset to ask, "Which or whose Bible is our authority?"

If then we know what and whose Bible has validity for us, the next question is, "By what authority can we say that these books are the Bible?" A Roman Catholic can appeal to the Council of Trent of 1546 and say that the contents of the scriptures were decided by fifty-three prelates with the concluding warning, "If however anyone does not receive the entire books with all their parts as they are accustomed to be read in the Catholic Church . . . let him be anathema." The Westminster Assembly of 1647, composed of Puritans who were influenced by the opinion of Calvinistic churches, formulated the Westminster Confession of Faith that defined the limits of the Bible. For the Old Testament, the contents were from Genesis to Malachi and for the New from Matthew to Revelation. Concerning the Apocrypha, the assembly affirmed that these books were not inspired and were not a part of the canon and had no value other than that of being human writings. Thus, the Presbyterians can resort to the Westminster Confession of Faith.

The Church of England has its declaration of scripture in the Thirty-nine Articles of 1562. Article six gives a precise statement about the contents of the Old Testament but no list of the New Testament books. Possibly the omission is due to an agreement with the Roman Catholic Church on the number of these documents. Relative to the Apocrypha, however, it concedes that these books may be read for example for life and instruction but not for establishing any doctrine. What about the Jews? What is their authority for the Jewish canon of thirty-nine books? They can call upon the Tannaitic rabbis of Jamnia who settled the matter for them around A.D. 90.[2]

Thus we see that the Roman Catholics, the Church of England, Presbyterians, and Reformed—as well as the Jews—can rest their case on some authority that determined the limits of the Bible. But as Baptists, to whom can we appeal for a decision relative to the contents of the scripture? Why not accept the Old Testament Apocrypha? Why not receive the apocryphal writings of the New Testament? Some will say, "I accept the Bible from Genesis to Revelation because my pastor, Sunday School teacher, or a friend taught me this." But what is the authority of those who taught you? Others might add, "Unless there is evidence to the contrary, I believe this because it is the sentiment that has always been expressed." In other words, the conviction is based strictly on tradition. This is not a wholesome answer, however, because tradition is not always reliable; some traditions contradict other traditions. Admittedly, the religious groups that have authoritatively announced what books are in the scriptures used tradition to make a final decision. In reality all Christians rely ultimately upon tradition no matter what a bishop, council, or assembly might have decreed.

Therefore, the purpose of this book is to explore the Jewish tradition surrounding the formation of the Old Testament and examine the criteria used by the Church Fathers for determining the list of the New Testament books. In this way the reader is no longer subjected to the opinion of an ecclesiastical official or the authoritative pronouncement of a church council. With the tradition set forth clearly, the reader can make an independent judgment on the value of the documents in both Testaments.

Frequently Christians refer to the Old Testament and New Testament as "the Book." The Bible is not a book, however, but a collection of books. The word "Bible" comes from the Greek word *biblia*, which is a neuter plural of *biblion* and means books or rolls. It is a library, the contents of which were written in places as far apart as Babylonia and Rome. The materials in the Bible cover a period of nearly a thousand years and embrace a variety of civilizations, cultures, social and economic changes, and transformed religious concepts. The various books constitute different types of literature: law, history, poetry, drama, prophetic oracles, apocalyptic imagery, Gospels, letters, and wisdom literature.

The two component parts of the Bible are actually misnomers. We should not say "Old Testament" and "New Testament." We ought to say "Old Covenant" and "New Covenant." We are so accustomed to these labels now, however, that it would be impossible to make the change. The Greek word *diathēkē* (covenant) can also mean a last will and testament and is so used in Galatians 3:15 and Hebrews 9:16f. When *diathēkē* was translated into Latin, the translators who were not very well acquainted with Judaism preferred the more legalistic meaning and used *testamentum*. Our first knowledge of Christians using "testament" in connection with both sections of the Bible comes from Tertullian, a presbyter of Carthage in North Africa, in the early years of the third century A.D. Actually Tertullian preferred the word *instrumentum* because it was more juristic and pleasing to his legal mindset.[3]

The two collections of sacred literature are in no sense a will or a testament. God's covenant with Israel was an agreement on the part of Israel to follow God's commands and be God's people. It was an agreement of God to be the God of Israel—provided Israel observed the divine commandments. It was a corporate relationship, not an individual one. For Christians, the new covenant is a relationship between God and the individual. Anyone who has faith in Christ comes into a right relationship with God and continues in this peaceful relationship.

We have referred previously to the canon of the New and Old Testaments. Now is the time to explain precisely what we mean when the term is used. The Greek word *kanon* originally meant a reed or measuring rod. It was a tool used by carpenters to determine the right direction of a piece of wood. Various metaphorical meanings were derived from this literal sense. Canon could be written laws of behavior, rules of philosophers or grammarians, an ecclesiastical ordinance passed by a council, a list of saints, an index table, or a list of books. We are using the word in the latter sense—a list of books that is specifically a collection of authoritative sacred literature. In a real sense canon cannot be used with the Old and New Testaments unless we mean a closed canon, that is, that the number of books is fixed and none can be added or deleted.

The notion of an exclusive selection of sacred books for public worship in the Christian church is derived from the Jews. The New Testament church is a church without a New Testament since the New Testament had not yet been formed. Therefore, it is necessary to consider the formation of the Old Testament first because it is in a way a model for the New Testament canon.

Notes

[1]The term Apocrypha is generally used to refer to a collection of writings that appeared in many ancient versions of the Old Testament and were widely used by early Christians but which later were largely excluded from the Bible by Protestants.

[2]After the destruction of Jerusalem by the Romans in A.D. 70, Jewish leaders drawn mostly from the ranks of the Pharisees established a center of learning near Joppa in order to preserve the Jewish religion and heritage. Scribal leaders of the group came to be known later as the Tannaim.

[3]Tertullian, *Against Marcion*, 4.1 and *Against Praxeas*, 15.

Chapter One

The Formation
of the Old Testament

The history of the Old Testament canon is not clear and distinct. It is generally conceded that the Jewish scriptures were canonized by three stages of development, corresponding to the three divisions of the Hebrew Bible. The Law (Torah), the first five books of the Old Testament, was canonized about 400 B.C. This dating is based largely on the approximate time the Samaritans split with the Jews and recognized only the Torah as scripture.

The section of the Hebrew Bible designated "Prophets" was finalized about 200 B.C. Evidence for this conclusion comes from *Jesus Ben Sira*, an apocryphal book on wisdom that was written about 180 B.C. In the author's praise of famous men, he extolled those who are included in the books of the Former Prophets (Joshua, Judges, 1 and 2 Samuel, and 1 and 2 Kings) and the Latter Prophets (Isaiah, Jeremiah, Ezekiel, and the Twelve [those we call the minor prophets]).[1]

The third section of the Hebrew scriptures, the "Writings," was known by 132 B.C. when the grandson of Jesus ben Sira translated his grandfather's book into Greek from the Hebrew. In his prologue to the translation, he said, "Whereas many great teachings have been given to us through the law and the prophets and the others" and then later "the law itself, the prophecies, and the rest of the books." He did not call the third section Writings, but he simply labeled the remaining books as "others" and "the rest."

We have reason to believe that the "Writings" in the day of Jesus Christ had not been closed as a part of the Hebrew Bible. If this part had been canonized, the debates among the rabbis in Jamnia with respect to certain of these documents would have no basis as to whether they did or did not *"defile the hands."* Presumably the Writings were still in a fluid state. On several occasions Jesus referred to "the law and the prophets" (Matt 5:17; 11:13; Luke 24:27), and in Luke 24:44 he spoke of "the law of Moses and the prophets and the Psalms." Psalms formed the opening and longest part of the "Writings" section. 1 and 2 Chronicles stand last in the order of books in the Hebrew canon; Jesus may have been acquainted with this when he said, "that upon you may come all the righteous blood shed on the earth, from the blood of Abel to the blood of Zechariah" (Matt 23:35). The account of Zechariah is found in 2 Chronicles 24:20-22, and the above statement of Jesus indicated he was reckoning from the first murder in Genesis to the last murder in the Old Testament.

The first three books of the last division of Hebrew scriptures are usually referred to as "poetical books." They are Psalms, Proverbs, and Job. They are followed by Song of Songs (Song of Solomon), Ruth, Lamentations, Ecclesiastes, and Esther. These five books stand together in the Hebrew canon and are called *Megilloth* (rolls or scrolls). Each one was read publicly at one of the annual festivals of the Jews: Song of Songs for the Feast of Passover, Ruth during Pentecost, Esther for the Feast of Purim (Lots), Ecclesiastes during the Feast of Tabernacles, and Lamentations for the Ninth of Ab in remembrance of the destruction of the temple by the Babylonians. To determine at what time the practice of the reading of these books for the above festivals began is impossible.

The last section of the Writings lists Daniel, 1 and 2 Chronicles, Ezra, and Nehemiah. It is interesting to note that Daniel does not stand with the Prophets in the Hebrew canon as it does in the Greek canon. This is because it was written about 165 B.C. after the division of the Prophets had been closed. Had Daniel been a prophetic book rather than an apocalyptic work, the Jews might have placed it with the Prophets.

The first witness to a fixed canon of the Old Testament was Josephus, the Jewish historian. Josephus had been a Sadducee, an Essene, and finally went over to the Pharisees. As a Sadducee he would have rejected all Jewish writings except the Torah (Law). As an Essene he would have accepted books other than those finalized in the Hebrew canon. As a Pharisee he included more books than the Sadducees and fewer than the Essenes.

Josephus, the Jewish historian, in his work *Against Apion* 1, 8, which was written about A.D. 93, said:

For we have not countless books among us, disagreeing from and contradicting one another (as the Greeks have), but only twenty-two books, which contain the records of all the past times; which are justly believed to be divine; and of them five belong to Moses, which contain his laws and the traditions of the origin of mankind till his death. . . . But as to the time from the death of Moses till the reign of Artaxerxes king of Persia, who reigned after Xerxes, the prophets who were after Moses wrote down what was done in their times in thirteen books. The remaining four books contain hymns to God and precepts for the conduct of human life.

Josephus went on to say that Jewish history had been written from the time of Artaxerxes, but it was not esteemed like the other because the succession of prophets had ceased. Josephus limited the books of the Old Testament to twenty-two probably to make the number conform to the letters of the Hebrew alphabet. He probably combined Ruth with Judges and Lamentation with Jeremiah. For the prophets he included (we assume) Joshua, Judges, Samuel, Kings, Isaiah, Jeremiah, Ezekiel, Daniel, the Twelve, Job, Chronicles, Ezra-Nehemiah, and Esther. As to the final four, our guess is that he had in mind Psalms, Proverbs, Ecclesiastes, and the Song of Songs. We note that in his *Antiquities* he used 1 Esdras from the Apocrypha rather than canonical Ezra-Nehemiah. In his presentation of Esther he inserted the name of God, which was not in the Hebrew text of this document but is found in the Greek additions to Esther.

What we find in this statement of Josephus is a time limit for the books of the Old Testament: from Moses to Artaxerxes I (who ruled from 464–423 B.C.) Books written after the time of Artaxerxes I were not given the same value by Josephus and other Jews because they believed that the prophetic chain was broken. How, then, could Josephus make this claim when he himself used 1 Esdras, a document of the second century B.C. in place of the document Ezra-Nehemiah in the Old Testament? He also apparently accepted Ruth and Jonah, which were written after the prescribed limits given above. Both of these books are an attack on the extreme nationalism and the separatist policy of Nehemiah and Ezra. Furthermore, Ecclesiastes, the Song of Songs, Daniel, Esther, and some of the Psalms were written as late as the third and second centuries B.C. and yet Josephus accepted them.

Was Josephus aware of the debates among the Pharisees at Jamnia concerning some of the books of the Old Testament? Was he in contact with the rabbis of Palestine after he was declared a traitor in the Rebellion of A.D. 66-70 when he surrendered the fortress of Jotapata so quickly to Vespasian and Titus? Though he was a Pharisee, it is not likely that the Pharisees would be on speaking terms with Josephus after he received an annual pension, a strip of land in Judea, and Roman citizenship from Vespasian. Furthermore, no evidence exists that Josephus ever returned to Palestine. Thus, it appears that he had no direct communication with the rabbis in Jamnia after the rebellion.

During the time that Josephus was writing his *Antiquities, Wars of the Jews,* and *Against Apion,* the rabbis in Jamnia were debating the merits of certain books in the Old Testament. After the destruction of Jerusalem in A.D. 70, Jamnia, near Joppa, became the center of the Sanhedrin. Johana ben Zakkai established the rabbinic academy there, and after his death he was succeeded by Gamaliel II. At Jamnia the formal fixing of the canon of the Old Testament occurred by means of discussions of the rabbis. Some scholars make the mistake of calling this the Council of Jamnia, though no formal council existed, and date it in A.D. 90. The debates among the rabbis continued from the founding of the Academy until the middle of the second century A.D.

The criteria used by the Jews for determining the limits of scripture prior to the discussions at Jamnia are unknown to us except for what we learn from Josephus. We can imagine they included contents of the books, usefulness for liturgical worship, practical wisdom, prophetic inspiration, divine instruction, and traditions linking the text to a revered ancestor as author. The principle for selecting the books at Jamnia in the first and second centuries A.D., however, is available for us in the Mishnah, the compilation of the rabbinical oral tradition by Jehuda ha-Nasi about A.D. 180. The rabbis introduced the nebulous criterion "defile the hands." What the expression meant, nobody knows. Those books that did not defile the hands were rejected. Perhaps this was a trick of the Pharisees to keep the Sadducees from interpreting the scriptures. The Pharisees could say that if the priests touched the sacred books, they would be defiled and could not perform their priestly duties and eat their priests' portion of the sacrifices. Later Judaism taught that the hands became unclean by contact with the Holy Scriptures so that the scriptures could not be touched with uncovered hands.[2] Sacredness was given to certain books and contact with anything sacred necessitated ablutions. If this was a ruse of the Pharisees, it was instituted prior to the destruction of Jerusalem and the temple, because after that time the Pharisees had full sway since the Sadducees lost their power with the demise of the temple cult.

The two books of the Old Testament that were debated most intensely by the rabbis at Jamnia were the Song of Songs and Ecclesiastes. Rabbi Simeon said that Ecclesiastes was rejected by the conservative school of Shammai, while the liberal school of Hillel declared that it was canonical.[3] He also said that Hillel accepted the Song of Songs, while Shammai rejected it. Akiba declared that all the Writings were holy, but the Song of Songs was the Holy of Holies. In the Babylonian Talmud Simon ben Menasya, a contemporary of Jehuda ha-Nasi, refused to accept Ecclesiastes because it was Solomon's own wisdom.[4] The rejection of this book by some rabbis may have been due to its pessimistic view of history.

The only way that Rabbi Akiba could possibly include the Song of Songs in the canon was by allegorizing it. He considered the bridegroom speaker in the twenty-five lyric poems to be Yahweh, who is the husband of his people Israel. Christians have also included this series of poems and allegorized them. Instead of Yahweh as husband of Israel, it is the love of Christ for his bride, the church. Without allegorizing the book, Christians could interpret it as nothing more than a myth connected with the love of a god and goddess in a fertility cult. The poems are full of sensuous and erotic imagery. Theodore, the bishop of Mopsuestia in Cilicia about A.D. 429, said that the Song of Songs did not mention the name of God. He also declared that it was not read by Jews or Christians publicly. He believed that the book tells of a wedding between Solomon and the daughter of Pharaoh. This wedding was not for pleasure but for political stability. The daughter of Pharaoh was black, and Solomon constructed a palace for her so that she would not be shunned in the harem. In order that he might not incur the wrath of Pharaoh he composed the Song of Songs.

While the book of Esther was not challenged in the Mishnah, rabbis rejected it in the third century A.D.[5] One of the problems with Esther was the feast of Purim, which was contrary to the Law (Lev 27:34). How could another feast be established when Moses had not enjoined such? In the Jerusalem Talmud we discover how the difficulty was overcome. The assertion is made there that the book of Esther was revealed to Moses on Mount Sinai but it was not written until the time of Esther and Mordecai. In A.D. 170 Melito, the bishop of Sardis, went to Palestine to get a list of the Old Testament books from the Jews, but it is quite noticeable that his list did not include Esther. It is also strange that, among the discoveries in the caves near the community of Qumran, fragments of every book of the Old Testament have been found with the exception of Esther. Did the community of Qumran exclude the book of Esther? Apparently it did. In his Festal Epistle of A.D. 367 Athanasius, the bishop of Alexandria, listed the books of the Old Testament and the New Testament; Esther did not fall within the listing. The fact that Greek additions were made to Esther to insert God into the book is a clear indication that a further objection was raised to the writing because it said nothing about God.

Possibly Esther, written after 200 B.C., was shaped to express the nationalistic zeal of the Jews that came from the Maccabean victories and especially the defeat of Nicanor. The first reference to the feast of Purim is found in 2 Maccabees 15:36; it is called Mordecai's day. Pfeiffer believes that the book of Esther was pure fiction and the feast of Nicanor that fell on the thirteenth of Adar was extended to the fourteenth and fifteenth days of Adar (the days of Purim) in order to express the popular patriotic enthusiasm of the Jews in celebration of Nicanor's day.[6]

In later Judaism, questions were raised concerning the validity of Proverbs and Ezekiel. Some rabbis wanted to exclude Proverbs from public reading because of the contradiction between 26:4 and 26:5. Verse 4 reads, "Answer not a fool according to his folly, lest you be like him yourself." Verse 5 removes the negative and says, "Answer a fool according to his folly, lest he be wise in his own eyes." The contradiction was settled by the rabbis by saying that verse 4 pertains to the discussions of the Law, while verse 5 has to do with worldly affairs.[7]

Though Ezekiel had been included among the Prophets since at least 200 B.C., certain rabbis said that the ending of Ezekiel did not agree with the Law. They also objected to the mystical teachings in chapters one through three, believing they might lead to theosophical speculations. A tradition in the Babylonian Talmud is recorded concerning Rabbi Hananiah, who burned 300 measures of oil night after night until he was able to reconcile the latter chapters of Ezekiel with the Law.

Also, three of the disputed books (Esther, Ecclesiastes, and Song of Songs) were in the "Rolls" section of the Writings. All three were documents read during a Jewish festival. Once these writings were associated in some way with a festival, it would have been extremely difficult to remove them.

Books other than the twenty-four in the Jewish canon acquired a measure of sanctity in some Jewish circles. Evidence for this comes from the discoveries at Qumran near the Dead Sea. Fragments from two books of the Apocrypha were found there. The book of Tobit is present in several copies, one in Hebrew and the others in Aramaic. Also among the finds were excerpts from Jesus ben Sira. In addition to these two documents contained in what we commonly call the Apocrypha were fragments of fourteen manuscripts of Jubilees, a few fragments of the Testament of the Twelve Patriarchs, and remains of eleven copies of 1 Enoch. The large amount of fragments from 1 Enoch and Jubilees would seem to indicate that the Qumran sect of Judaism accepted these books as sacred literature.

If the author of 2 Esdras can be trusted, we learn that there were seventy books not included in the Old Testament canon. These were not to be read publicly but were to be given to the wise because they contained esoteric doctrines. The author concluded, however, with this statement: "For in them is the spring of understanding, the fountain of wisdom, and the river of knowledge." The seventy documents must have included the technical Apocrypha and other works commonly designated Pseudepigrapha. 2 Esdras was written at the close of the first century A.D. and is an apocalyptic work, at least chapters three through fourteen.

Whether the Jews outside Palestine accepted a wider list of books than the Palestinian rabbis is still a matter of intense debate. Some contend that the diaspora Jews had an Alexandrian (originated in Alexandria, Egypt) canon that included the Apocrypha. Although this belief might be true, no firm evidence supports this claim. We know that Jesus ben Sira was translated into Greek in Egypt by the author's grandson, and that the Wisdom of Solomon was probably written in Greek in Egypt as well. The Additions to Daniel and 2 Maccabees appear to have been written in Greek, but the remaining books of the Apocrypha were probably originally in Hebrew or Aramaic and translated into Greek. Possibly, the collection of these books, begun by the Jews, gained a degree of sanctity, but the debates on the Jewish canon at Jamnia stopped the action.

Christians took over the Jewish apocryphal writings since they were not bound by the rabbinic decisions at Jamnia. With the exception of the fragments discovered at Qumran, the manuscripts that contain the

Apocrypha are Christian manuscripts. These uncial Greek manuscripts are Sinaiticus (4th cent. A.D.), Vaticanus (4th cent. A.D.), Alexandrius (5th cent. A.D.), and Ephraemi (5th cent. A.D.). The divisions of the Hebrew canon are ignored in these Christian copies, and the books of the Old Testament and the Apocrypha are distributed throughout the collection without any clear rhyme or reason.

The rabbis at Jamnia, with the exception of a general statement from Akiba and a specific reference to Jesus ben Sira, seemed to remain silent about these books outside the Jewish canon. In the Mishnah, Rabbi Akiba, who flourished in the middle half of the second century A.D. said that whoever read the external books (those outside the canon) had no share in the life to come. In the Tosefta (a collection of oral tradition paralleling the Mishnah), we learn that the book of Jesus ben Sira and books written since that time "do not defile the hands."[8]

While the New Testament contains only one clear quotation from the apocryphal writings, some passages reflect or allude to the documents. The Wisdom of Solomon (7:26, 5:17; 9:15; 13-15) is reflected in Hebrews 1:3, Ephesians 6:11 and 13, 2 Corinthians 5:4, and Romans 1:18-2:24, respectively. Hebrews 11:35-36 makes an allusion to 2 Maccabees 6-7. Jerome said that Matthew 27:9 was from the apocryphal work Jeremiah, and Origen stated that 1 Corinthians 2:9 was from the Apocalypse of Elijah. In Jude we find a quotation from 1 Enoch and an allusion to the Assumption of Moses. Jannes and Jambres are cited in 2 Timothy 3:9 as those who were opposed to Moses, yet they are not mentioned in Exodus. Did this reference come from the Jewish oral tradition, or was it from an apocryphal document? In addition to the reflections and allusions above, unknown works are cited in Luke 11:49, John 7:38, Ephesians 5:14, and James 4:5. These are either paraphrases of an Old Testament text, or they come from apocryphal writings.

Did the rabbis at Jamnia act on their own initiative in fixing the canon of the Old Testament, or did they consider the popular opinion based on usage of the documents? We do not know. What justifiable reason could the officials of the rabbinical academy give for rejecting 1 Maccabees and accepting Esther? Why did they exclude Jesus ben Sira and the Wisdom of Solomon and include Ecclesiastes? 1 Maccabees is the most fascinating book in Israel's romantic history. It tells of dedicated and faithful Jews who were willing to die for the Law. Even if we take the book only for its historic interest, it is very significant because Antiochus

Epiphanes was determined to blot out Judaism. If we compare the wisdom of Jesus ben Sira or the Wisdom of Solomon with Ecclesiastes, we will perceive that the wisdom of the former overshadows the latter.

The failure of the Apocrypha to achieve a place in the Hebrew canon could hardly have been based on its intrinsic value. If indeed this were the case, a large segment of the Old Testament would have been eliminated. Can we rely upon the vague "defile the hands" criterion that dominated the decisions of the Jamnia rabbis? Shall we dare to engage in debate with the same freedom as the Tannaitic teachers who argued pro and con on the status of Esther, Song of Songs, Ecclesiastes, Proverbs, and Ezekiel, or shall we consider the matter closed? We must test the Hebrew canon and the wider canon that includes the Apocrypha on our own and determine the validity of the books incorporated in this collection.

The Jewish canon did not enjoy validity in the early Church. Its authority was not actually assessed until the Reformation, and even then the apocryphal works were united with the Jewish canon as an appendix to the Old Testament. In the early fifth century A.D., Jerome, in his Latin translation of the Bible known as the Vulgate, excluded the Apocrypha and accepted only the Jewish canon. Later at the Council of Trent in 1546, the fifty-three representatives reversed the decision of Jerome and made the Apocrypha equal to the Old Testament. The decision, however, was not so binding on Roman Catholics so as to keep some scholars from expressing doubts concerning the Apocrypha's equal status with the Old Testament. The rejection of these writings has not been universal and absolute among Protestants.

Notes

1. Jesus ben Sira, chaps. 44-49.
2. Babylonian Talmud, Shabbath 14a.
3. Mishnah, Eduyoth 5.3 and Yadaim 3.5.
4. Babylonian Talmud, Megillah 7a.
5. Ibid., Sanhedrin 110b and Megillah 7a.
6. Robert H. Pfeiffer, *Introduction to the Old Testament* (New York: Harper & Brothers, 1941) 745.
7. Ibid., Shabbath 30b.
8. Tosefta, Yadaim 2.3.

Chapter Two

The Formation
of the New Testament in
the West

When, where, and under what circumstances did the twenty-seven books of the New Testament become a sacred collection? These questions must be considered in any study of the canon of the New Testament. The sources for this study are more abundant and more clearly defined than the sources for the Old Testament canon.

The books of the New Testament, like those of the Old, were recognized as worthy of being elevated to the rank of scripture only after a long period of time. The Bible of Jesus and the apostles was the Old Testament. Our knowledge of the historical Jesus has never been centered in something that he wrote. We have no evidence that he commissioned his disciples to publish his teachings except for the statement of Tertullian, which has no foundation. The early disciples were more interested in the transmission of the Good News by means of oral tradition. They were awed and astonished by the words, deeds, and presence of Jesus. They had witnessed his resurrection, and by that event they recognized that he was Lord, equated with Yahweh (a Hebrew name for God) of the Old Testament. Such astonishment cannot be captured in writing. It became more alive by communicating to others through word of mouth.

Christianity has established itself as a major religion in the world, not so much by reason of books or the Bible being read from generation to generation, for millions of Christians for the past nearly 2000 years could not read. In fact, multitudes today cannot read, but this does not disqualify them from the Christian community. They have had an experience with the living Christ just as those who read. A father or a mother tells the Good News to a child, a friend tells a friend, a minister proclaims the message of Christ to his hearers, and as a result people believe. Of course, there is always the danger of more errors in the oral tradition because no external standard exists by which to measure what is taught. An equal danger comes from the written tradition when it becomes a "book" religion.

During the first hundred years of Christianity when the Christians spoke of "the scripture" or "the scriptures," they had in mind the Jewish sacred body of literature. As we have mentioned before, the Old Testament was still in a fluid state. Certain books in the "Writings" section were questioned in the discussions at Jamnia. The chief interest of the early Christians in the Old Testament revolved around the prophets and psalms because in them they could find predictions about events and the messiah, which were fulfilled in Jesus Christ. All of the books that now form our New Testament were written in this period of time, and even quoted by the early Church Fathers. There is no evidence that these documents were considered to be a second sacred collection of literature having equal standing with the scriptures inherited from the Jews.

Hints in the Gospels, Acts, and epistles show a movement in the direction of a new sacred body of literature. For example, the words of Jesus were an antitheses to the words from the Old Testament (Matt 5:21-48); Paul appealed to the words of Jesus for his authority (Acts 20:35; 1 Thess 4:15; 1 Cor 11:23); Paul claimed to have a revelation not found in the apostolic tradition (1 Cor 7:10); Paul requested that his letters be read in the churches (1 Thess 5:27; Col 4:16); Paul appealed to apostolic authority for sound teaching in the Pastorals (1 Tim. 6:3; 2 Tim 1:13,14); and the statement in 2 Peter indicates that Paul's letters had been elevated to a position of authority (3:16).

Some scholars assume that if the early Church Fathers referred to or quoted from a document of the New Testament that this was equivalent to classifying it as scripture. They use quotations from Clement of Rome, Ignatius, Polycarp, Justin Martyr, the *Didache*, the *Shepherd of Hermas*, the *Epistle of Barnabas,* and others to justify their position. We must bear in mind, however, that these are free quotations, and that some of them could have come from the oral tradition. Our concern has to do with the date and place at which a writing takes on scriptural proportions making it equal to if not superior to the scriptures of the Old Testament.

When the above Church Fathers wrote, the oral tradition was to some more important than anything written. According to Eusebius, Papias, the bishop of Hierapolis, wrote five books entitled *An Exposition of the Oracles of the Lord*. In this work Papias tells us that the Gospels of Matthew and Mark were current in his time. Of the former he said, "Matthew composed the oracles in Hebrew, and each one interpreted them as he was able." Of the latter he said that the Elder (John) used to say, "Mark, having become Peter's interpreter, wrote accurately all that he remembered." Apparently he was not satisfied with written documents because he sought after words from the elders concerning what Andrew, Peter, Philip, Matthew, James, John, and others said in the past and what Aristion and the Elder John said in the present. Papias went on to say, "For I did not account it that the things from the books were to me of so much profit as the things from a living and remaining voice."[1] Eusebius also said that Papias quoted from 1 John and 1 Peter. The fact that Papias believed that the kingdom of Christ would exist on the earth for a thousand years leads us to believe he was acquainted with the book of Revelation.

Papias was an older contemporary of Polycarp, so he must have been born around A.D. 80. Some suggest that he was a pagan by birth. Papias was a friend of Polycarp, the bishop of Smyrna. Unlike Polycarp, who told the Philippians that they could be built up in the faith by reading Paul's letters, Papias was silent about Paul. Surely he knew of a collection of Paul's letters. Possibly, he did not agree with Paul's teachings. At any rate, we learn from an ecclesiastical official of the East, who flourished between A.D. 125–150, that oral tradition was more highly revered than documents.

Justin Martyr

Justin Martyr marks the era of transition from the oral tradition to the written tradition. The date of his birth is uncertain, but it was probably at the close of the first century. Justin was of Greek parentage, and his family had settled in the Roman colony of Flavia Neapolis near the site of ancient Shechem in Samaria. In his *Dialogue with Trypho*, he related how he sought truth among the philosophical schools of his day. He was a Stoic, Peripatetic, Pythagorean, and Platonist. At last he met an old man who told him about Christianity. He was thrilled to discover that this was the only safe and useful philosophy.

Three genuine works of Justin have been preserved, two *Apologies* and the *Dialogue with Trypho*. The first *Apology* is a defense of Christianity sent to Emperor Antioninus Pius between A.D. 138–161. The second Apology was addressed to the Roman Senate between A.D. 144 and 160. The *Dialogue with Trypho* is a series of discussions with a Jew whom Justin met in the public walk at Ephesus. In the debates with Trypho he tried to prove from the Old Testament that Jesus was the messiah. At Rome Justin established a school where he sought to convert Greeks by his persuasive powers as a philosopher. He remained in Rome until his martyrdom in A.D. 165 under Marcus Aurelius.

While most of the quotations in Justin's writings are from the Old Testament, a mass of references embrace the chief facts about Jesus' life and many details of his teaching, which he said are contained in the *Memoirs of the Apostles*. Justin did not mention any authors connected with the *Memoirs*. These references for the most part coincide with the material found in Matthew, Mark, and Luke (more related to Matthew). Some of his quotations seem to be from memory rather than from written documents. A few of Justin's citations come from gospels that are apocryphal in nature. He said that Jesus was born in a cave, that the wise men were from Arabia, and that Jesus made ploughs and yokes as a carpenter. In the past some have suggested that he made use of the *Gospel of the Hebrews* or the *Gospel of Peter*, but at the present time few would agree to this. In addition to *Memoirs of the Apostles,* to which Justin referred eight times, and the shortened form *Memoirs*, which he cited four times, he mentioned the book of Revelation and named the author as John, one of the apostles of Christ.

In his Apology to Emperor Pius, Justin said that on the day called the Sun some Christians gathered and read the *Memoirs* and the Prophets.[2] Did he mean that the *Memoirs* were read in the weekly services of the church on equal footing as the Prophets, or does the order in which he presented them suggest that the *Memoirs* were placed above the Prophets? In either case, the *Memoirs* were elevated to the rank of scripture.

Why was Justin so silent about the letters of Paul? Although he used some of the Old Testament passages in his disputations with Trypho that Paul had used in his letters, he did not refer to any document in the Pauline collection. Was it because of his dislike of Marcion, a contemporary in Rome, who distrusted the apostolic tradition and said that Paul preached the genuine gospel? This is quite possible.

Tatian

Tatian was one of the most influential students of Justin Martyr. Born somewhere in Assyria and reared as a Greek, he studied philosophy just as his teacher had. In his *Oration to the Greeks* he told how hollow and foul he had found Greek philosophies and their mystery cults to be. At last he encountered documents more ancient than the Greeks, and his search for truth had ended. (We do not know at what time of his life this occurred.) Without a doubt, the documents were of the Old Testament and possibly the Gospels. Tatian came to Rome as a pagan, but under the influence of Justin he became a Christian. After the death of Justin in A.D. 165, Tatian took Justin's place as teacher. About A.D. 172, he broke with the church in Rome and returned to the East. Some say that he never completely severed his connection with the church. In the East he became a leader of an ascetic group called the Encratites. The title of the movement comes from the Greek *enkrates* ("self-controlled")found in Titus 1:8. The Encratites abolished marriage, drinking wine, and eating meat. Like the Marconites and Montanists, they sought the satisfaction of their peculiar needs in a system of strict discipline and stern logic.

Tatian was probably influenced by Marcion because he had a high regard for Paul's letters, though Jerome two centuries later said that Tatian rejected some of them. We do know that he rejected 1 and 2 Timothy because of the encouragement to use wine in 1 Timothy 5:23 and the rejection of ascetic views in 4:1. However, he thought Titus was a genuine letter of Paul. In this respect he accepted one of the Pastorals, but it is to be noted that Marcion rejected all of them. Instead of one Gospel (Luke) in Marcion's canon, Tatian upheld the primacy of four Gospels. His greatest achievement was his *Diatessaron,* which was a weaving together of the four Gospels into one. *Diatessaron* is a Greek word that means "by means of four." Apparently the *Diatessaron* is the first recognition of a fourfold gospel. In the fifth century A.D., Theodoret, bishop of Cyrus in upper Syria, said that Tatian removed the genealogies from his composition, and Theodoret accused him of evil intent in this act. He found over 200 copies of Tatian's work in Syria and had them banned. In their place he introduced the separated Gospels.

It is unknown whether Tatian was acquainted with Marcion during his stay in Rome, but his interest in Paul's letters and his ascetic views would seem to indicate that he was. He was unlike Marcion, however, in that he included not just one Gospel but all four Gospels in his canon. Irenaeus, who had a supersensitive nose that could smell the odor of heresy in every puff of wind, accused Tatian of heresy.

Now we enter that period of the history of Christianity when the Church Fathers had to make a selection of Christian writings because certain movements were afoot that might spell disaster for the community of believers. Thus we are summoned to ask certain questions. Unfortunately, the answers to these questions are not forthcoming, but in our study we shall probably pick up hints that might suggest a solution. Why are there four Gospels—"no more and no less?" When Luke wrote, he was aware that many had undertaken the tasks of writing a narrative about Jesus (1:1). We also have evidence of other gospels by name: the *Gospel of the Hebrews*, the *Gospel of the Egyptians*, the *Gospel of Peter*, the *Gospel of Philip*, the *Gospel of Thomas*, the *Gospel of Truth*, and the *Gospel of the Twelve Apostles*. Why are there so many of Paul's epistles? Why do we have only one book of Acts? There were others: the *Acts of Peter*, the *Acts of Paul*, the *Acts of John*, the *Acts of Pontius Pilate*, the *Acts of Andrew*, and the *Acts of Thomas*. Why do we not have more books written by apostles? Why does Luke have such a large portion of the New Testament? Why is there only one book of Revelation? We know of a book of Revelation by Peter. Finally, what is the relationship between the Old Testament and the New Testament?

Several theories have been advanced to account for the sifting of the mass of Christian writings to form the New Testament. Some would suggest that this selection was by the power of the Holy Spirit in a supernatural and mysterious manner. Such a supposition, however, is immediately abandoned when we review the pages of patristic literature. Others might believe that the selection of the New Testament books was accomplished in a democratic way. This belief is far from the truth. No vote secured the popular approval of the Christian communities. If the democratic process had prevailed, we would have a different New Testament. Some documents were more popular than those canonized. The *Shepherd of Hermas* was probably more admired and widely read than any other book. The *Didache*, the *Epistle of Barnabas*, the *Revelation of Peter*, the *Gospel of the Egyptians*, the *Epistle of Clement*, and the *Gospel of Peter* were also very popular in certain circles. Putting the matter to a vote makes us feel more comfortable in that all Christians took part in the selection process. If we investigate on our own, we will discover that the sifting of documents was done by men whose ecclesiastical position placed them on a level of authority with the New Testament writers themselves.

Still others will say that the Roman Catholic Church gave us the New Testament. Yet the documents were in existence before the Roman Catholic Church. It would have been more advantageous for the Catholic Church to discard the New Testament and resort to its dogma that revelation was continued through apostolic succession. Nevertheless, the books were there, and the church had no choice but to accept them; the New Testament has been a source of trouble for the Roman Catholic Church ever since. When the twenty-seven books of the New Testament were finally canonized, the voice of Rome did not make the decision. In his Easter letter to all Christendom, Althanasius, bishop of Alexandria, became the first to finalize the New Testament. The Third Council of Carthage in A.D. 397 followed the lead of Athanasius and declared that the twenty-seven books constituted the second collection of sacred literature. In A.D. 419 the decrees from the council were sent to Pope Boniface in Rome, not for his approval but only for information.

In the middle of the second century A.D., the books of the New Testament were mingled with a mass of other Christian literature (Gospels, apocalypses, sermons, epistles, prophecies, and histories). This literature was very popular with the majority of Christians. Prior to this time no effort had been made to sift this material and establish the boundary lines between the accepted and unaccepted writings. As we have previously noted, Papias, bishop of Hierapolis who died about A.D. 160, preferred the oral tradition of the words of Jesus to the written documents. Prior to the middle of the second century and continuing for years thereafter, however, certain movements that disrupted the unity of the church were initiated by teachers who were considered unorthodox in their views. These movements led to a lack of trust in the oral tradition and reversed the opinion of Papias.

Marcion

One of the movements that caused great alarm and much consternation among the ecclesiastical leaders was started by Marcion. Marcion was a shipbuilder from Sinope of the province of Pontus in Asia Minor. Tradition has it that his father was the bishop of Sinope. Marcion migrated to Rome between A.D. 140–150. According to Tertullian, Marcion gave a huge sum of money to the church of Rome. In Rome he was influenced by Cerdo, the Syrian Gnostic. Through the influence of Cerdo, he observed a great discrepancy between the God of the Old Testament and the God revealed in Jesus Christ. He interpreted the Old Testament literally and could not reconcile the character of God revealed in this literature with the revelation of God in Jesus Christ. Others had no problem with this discrepancy because they used the allegorical method of interpretation. Marcion refused to resort to this method. Today scholars could bring relief to Marcion by pointing out that what is not consistent with the revelation of God in Jesus Christ is not of God but is a failure of Israel to comprehend clearly God's revealing activity.

Marcion was the first Christian to reject the Old Testament. Up to this time the Christian community had relied heavily on the Old Testament, especially the prophets and Psalms, for proof texts that foretold the coming of Jesus. By repudiating the Jewish heritage of Christianity, Marcion removed the literature that had been considered scripture. He then proceeded to limit the documents of the church, the first person to do so. He introduced the first closed canon of distinctively Christian writings.

The canon of Marcion included one Gospel and ten epistles of Paul. The Gospel that he chose was Luke; though he did not call it the Gospel of Luke, but we know from Irenaeus and Tertullian that this is the one he used. Apparently he considered it more reliable because the author was closely associated with Paul. Marcion's enemies said that he mutilated the Gospel of Luke, extracting all elements in the document that pertained to the Old Testament and Judaism. For him the Gospel began with the third chapter. Thus, he omitted the birth narratives of John the Baptist and Jesus and left out the genealogy of Jesus in chapter 3. By limiting the number of Paul's epistles to ten, he ignored the Pastorals (1 Timothy, 2 Timothy, and Titus). Did he know these letters and omit them, or was he unaware of them? Today a majority of scholars believe that these letters were written under the name of Paul using fragments of Paul's epistles still found in 2 Timothy and Titus as a framework for the compositions. What Marcion called the letter to the Laodiceans we know as Ephesians. Possibly, he had the correct destination for the epistle, since the earlier copies of Ephesians do not name its recipients.

Marcion was accused by his enemies of corrupting the text of Paul's epistles. They said that he contended that Jewish Christians had tampered with the text to bring the apostle more in line with adherence to the law. No doubt that Marcion made changes, but his motive was to purify the documents from interpolations. The shipbuilder from Pontus intended to restore the gospel to a pure Pauline basis. His point of departure was the teaching of a Pauline antithesis, an antithesis between faith and works, gospel and law, and the children of wrath and the children of grace. He also sought to cut off any attempt in the future to corrupt the stream of tradition.

Marcion has been accused of being a Gnostic, but he was far from being related to this group because he stressed faith, as did Paul, and not knowledge, which was supported by the Gnostics. Furthermore, he did not resort to speculative theology and philosophy as did the Gnostics and the ecclesiastical leaders. Marcion had no esoteric and exoteric teachings to propound. He was not a philosopher but a reformer.

Though Marcion did not understand Paul's reason for preserving the Old Testament—despite the fact that the law was no longer of any value—he did grasp the profound principle of Paul that a right relationship with God was based on faith in Jesus Christ, a principle that the church of his day had lost. Marcion was the first person since Paul to raise the question of the relationship of the Old Testament to the New; Christendom has been trying to answer the question from that time forward. Also, Marcion was the first to make an earnest attempt to fix the boundaries of Christian documents and to exalt a definite collection of writings to the plane of canonical authority. Thus, we can say without equivocation that Marcion, who was classified as a heretic by the church, was the first to set forth a canon of the New Testament.

Marcion was very influential in Rome, all of Italy, Arabia, Syria, Armenia, Cyprus, Egypt, and perhaps Persia. His movement continued for centuries and finally came to an end in the seventh century under the name of the Paulicians. His teachings led to a fiery reaction from the ecclesiastical leaders of his day. Polycarp, the bishop of Smyrna, called him "the first born of Satan." Justin Martyr, the first Christian apologist and a martyr for his faith under the Emperor Marcus Aurelius about A.D. 165, said of Marcion: "By the help of devils he has caused many of every nation to speak blasphemies, and to deny that God is the maker of the universe" (*1 Apology* 26). In his writings against heresies, Irenaeus, the bishop of Lyons in Gaul, took licks at Marcion, but he looked upon the Gnostics as the greatest foe to Christianity. Tertullian, a presbyter from Carthage in North Africa and a contemporary of Irenaeus, was far more vitriolic and extremely caustic in his denunciations of Marcion than any other ecclesiastical leader.

Tertullian wrote five books against Marcion. He began by blasting Pontus, the province of his birth. He said that Pontus was inhabited by the fiercest of people who were nomads and had no fixed abode. There was no germ of civilization in the land because the people ran around naked. Women uncovered their breasts, from which they suspended their battle axes, and they preferred war to marriage. He went on to say that the natives of Pontus cut up the dead bodies of their parents with the sheep and ate them at feasts. He vividly described the extremely cold winters and hot summers of the area and finally concluded that the worst inhabitant that came out of this uncivilized province was Marcion, the Pontic mouse, who gnawed at the scriptures until nothing was left. Evidently from the above quotations, Marcion was not held in high esteem by the church.

Another movement prevalent in the second century was Christian Gnosticism. One branch of Gnosticism had its origin in Asia Minor and was associated with Cerenthus. The other branch, which was the greatest threat to the Christian faith, arose in Egypt and spread to Rome and other parts of Italy. Leaders of this Gnostic movement were Basilides, Valentinus, Heracleon, and Ptolemaeus. Our knowledge of these men is very limited, but what we do know of them has come to us, as in the case of Marcion, from their most bitter opponents. In the collection of fifty-two Nag Hammadi documents, discovered in 1945 in Upper Egypt, possibly two were written by Valentinus, the *Gospel of Truth* and the *Epistle to Rheginus on Resurrection*. The *Gospel of Truth* was not a rival Gospel, for Irenaeus said that it was only a manifesto of the Valentinian school. If, indeed, Valentinus was the author of these two documents, we have further knowledge of Valentinus and his followers.[3]

The Gnostics used the written tradition to set forth a metaphysical system based on Stoic, Platonist, Neo-Pythagorean, and Neo-Platonic elements of Greek philosophy. They believed that the deep mysteries of Christianity were available only to the learned. Salvation came through knowledge (*gnosis*) and not by faith in Christ. Knowledge consisted in the awareness of how the universe was created, the understanding of the plight of humanity, the know-how of salvation, and acquaintance with the ultimate destiny of mankind. The Gnostics used the allegorical method of interpretation, so diligently followed by the Jew Philo in the interpretation of the Old Testament, to set forth grotesque ideas from the Gospels and epistles that the writers never imagined. They let their minds run wild, and their system of speculative theology was mind boggling.

Basilides was possibly from Alexandria, Egypt, and—according to Clement of Alexandria—lived during the time Hadrian was emperor (A.D. 117–138). Basilides appealed to the authority of Glaucias, who he said was an interpreter of Peter. Tradition has it that he wrote twenty-four books of exegesis on the Gospel. Origin said that he had the boldness to write a Gospel and give it his own name. Valentinus was from Alexandria, but he went to Rome and was probably there when Marcion was expounding his views. While Basilides got his authority from Peter through Glaucias, Valentinus claimed his authority through Theodas, who he said was a disciple of Paul. If we were certain that the *Gospel of Truth* found at Nag Hammadi in 1945 is truly the work of Valentinus, the citations from the New Testament are so extensive in the treatise that we are obliged to affirm that he considered the documents authoritative. He and others of his school never referred to the New Testament books cited as scripture, unlike Basilides.

Clement of Alexandria said that the most influential of all the followers of Valentinus was Heracleon, who probably taught in a city in southern Italy. We are interested in Heracleon because he wrote the first commentary on John's Gospel. In the fragment that we have of Origen's commentary on John in the third century, the commentary of Heracleon is referred to more than sixty times. In this commentary on John by Origen, he agreed many times with Heracleon. He did not object to his allegorical method of interpretation. He regarded it as perfectly legitimate. Rather he objected to the theology Heracleon fostered in his interpretation. Another disciple of Valentinus wrote a commentary on the prologue to John's Gospel. His work was prior to that of Heracleon.

A third movement in the second century A.D., Montanism, had a direct bearing on shaping the new body of sacred literature. Montanus, a pagan priest from Phrygia, was converted to Christianity. He believed that he was the mouthpiece of the Holy Spirit and delivered utterances in a state of ecstasy. Among his followers were two women by the names of Maximilla and Priscilla. He taught that the end of the age was near, and that Jesus would come again and set up a kingdom on earth in Phrygia, not Jerusalem. The aim of Montanus was to recover the spirit of prophecy that had been so prominent in the early church.

Against the worldliness and decline of moral standards in the Christian communities becoming secularized, Montanus preached a rigid asceticism. Against a growing sacerdotalism of the church, he taught a universal priesthood of believers that included females. He championed the right of each individual to perform functions related to the ministry of the church. In this he was hostile to the centralization of power in the episcopate. Montanus insisted that God alone, by the endowment of the Holy Spirit, made ministers. This claim was made in opposition to human ordination.

The teaching of Montanus that concerns us more in this study is his emphasis on the continuance of prophecy. If a person should ask him what was the New Testament, he would say, "I do not know, it hasn't been revealed to me." His New Testament was the latest revelation from the Holy Spirit. It was not bound up in a volume but based on the latest news from God. In a word, it was the newest Testament. This sort of doctrine could play havoc for those who tried to define the limits of the written documents of the Christian faith. A continuing revelation counteracts the notion of a closed canon. We shall notice later that Tertullian sought to be a Catholic and a Montanist, but the principles of the two are as irreconcilable as anarchy and monarchy.

Montanism was never considered a heresy in the regular sense. Montanus was not as much concerned with theology as he was for the Christian way of living and stern discipline. The Montanists accepted the Church doctrine, so they were orthodox. If they had been able to wage their battle on the moral issue alone, they might have succeeded in Christendom. Their purity of conduct, the stern demands they made upon their followers, and the joy demonstrated in martyrdom elevated them above the average members of the Christian community. In this respect they were very apostolic. The word apostolic, however, was beginning to take on a new meaning—that of holding a deposit of pure doctrine.

The onslaught of the movements led by Marcion, the Christian Gnostics, and Montanus threatened the unity of the church. The ecclesiastical leaders who had made no statement about the limits of the books of the New Testament had to make a judgment because the Gnostics contended for many Gospels and Marcion supported only the Gospel of Luke. On what basis could they add to Marcion and subtract from the Gnostics? No council or ecclesiastical official before Marcion and the Gnostics had given an authoritative list of the New Testament books. No one had suggested that these books and these alone constituted a second sacred body of literature. Then, too, with Montanus' view of a continuing revelation there could never be a closed list of books.

How could the church refute Marcion and the Gnostics and at the same time contain Montanus? Who had the true interpretation of the Old and New Testaments? Who occupied the chairs of the apostles and had the right to give clear guidance to believers? Had some of the Church Fathers of the past confronted disorders and confusions that upset the unity of the Christian fellowship?

In the last decade of the first century A.D. Clement, the bishop of Rome, sent a letter to the church in Corinth scolding the Corinthians for deposing the old clergymen and replacing them with new men. He claimed that his letter was inspired, and he begged the congregation to restore order and unity within the church. He also urged them to rectify the scandal that they caused in deposing members of the sacred order who were in due succession from the apostles. In the early part of the second century, Ignatius, the bishop of Antioch, solved the problem of disunity by declaring that the local bishop was the focus of unity. Apart from the bishop the sacraments could not be administered; the bishop was God's representative on earth. Ignatius said, "We ought to regard the bishop as the Lord himself!"

The authority of the bishop proposed by Ignatius and the succession of apostles propounded by Clement were the weapons available to Irenaeus and Tertullian in the last quarter of the second century in their attack on Marcion and the Gnostics. They both contended that they were in the apostolic succession, whereas the Gnostics and Marcion were not. They ordered these heretics, who were using the same books of the New

Testament as they used, to get off their territory. In the work of Tertullian, *The Prescription of Heretics* 37, he said:

> Not being Christians, they have acquired no right to the Christian scrip-
> tures. It may be very fairly said to them, "Who are you? When and
> from where did you come? As you are none of mine, what have you to
> do with what is mine? Indeed, Marcion, by what right do you hew my
> wood? By whose permission, Valentinus, are you diverting the streams
> of my fountain? By what power, Apelles, are you removing my land-
> marks? This is my property. I have possessed it. I possessed it before
> you. I hold sure title-deeds from the original owners themselves, to
> whom the estate belonged. I am the heir of the apostles. Just as they
> carefully prepared their last will and testament and committed it as a
> trust, even so do I hold it."

Prominent in this statement is the dictatorial "I." Tertullian said that this
book is "mine," and that you are trespassing on "my" property. You are
diverting "my" streams and removing "my" landmarks.

History is full of overstatements, and those who make them are finally forced to modify them. Such a case in point is that of Tertullian, "that
the *Evangelical Testament* (*Evangelium Instrumentum*) has apostles for
its authors, to whom was assigned by the Lord himself this office of publishing the gospel."[4] This was the first time such a claim had been made.
Also, Tertullian restricted the office of apostle to the Twelve in spite of
the fact that the title was still being used in connection with the seventy
and for men like Paul, Barnabas, and Clement of Rome.

Through Irenaeus and Tertullian the apostolic standard became the
criterion for determining what documents should be placed in the second
authoritative sacred body of literature. They were, however, confronted
with the question, "Who wrote the Gospels?" Before the latter half of the
second century we have few references to the Gospels by name. Eusebius, the church historian of the fourth century, gave a tradition of
Papias, the bishop of Hierapolis, in the first half of the second century
who said that Matthew drew up a collection of the sayings of Jesus in the
Hebrew dialect and that "every one translated it as he was able."[5] He also
said that Mark was the interpreter of Peter and wrote all that he remembered from Peter's preaching about the sayings and the doings of the
Lord.[6] If Papias knew of Luke or John, he was silent on the matter. In
the second half of the second century, Justin Martyr, in his *Dialogue with*

Trypho mentioned the *Memoirs* of Peter and in his *First Apology* referred to the *Memoirs of the Apostles*. In church services these memoirs, also called Gospels, were read along with the prophets. Justin used traditions about Jesus not contained in the four Gospels. Apparently he received these from apocryphal Gospels.

Tatian, a student of Justin, took the four Gospels and joined them together in a continuous narrative and composed what was called the *Diatessaron* (by means of four). It was probably written in Greek and later translated into Syriac. Until the standardized Syriac text (*Peshitta*) was established in the early part of the fifth century, the *Diatessaron* and the Old Testament constituted the Bible for the Syrian church. The *Diatessaron* of Tatian bears witness to the fact that the sole interest in the Gospels was the life and works of Jesus, which they revealed, rather than a concern for literary authorship. We have noted that Marcion accepted only the Gospel of Luke. (He did not say that Luke wrote it.) We have also noted that the Gnostics used apocryphal Gospels to support their views.

While authorship of the Gospels heretofore had not been an engrossing question, it became a serious matter of concern for Irenaeus. He even attempted to state the order in which the Gospels were written. He listed Matthew first and then Mark, possibly following the tradition of Papias. Then he said that Luke, a companion of Paul, recorded the gospel preached by Paul. Finally, he says that John, the disciple of the Lord, who also leaned upon his breast, published a Gospel while living in Ephesus in Asia.[7] A little later in his book he fixed the number of the Gospels on numerological principles. He said that there were no more than four and no less than four. In saying that there were no more than four Gospels, Irenaeus was attacking the Gnostics for including apocryphal Gospels. When he said no less than four he had in mind Marcion, who accepted only the mutilated Gospel of Luke.

The reasoning on the part of Irenaeus for there being four and only four Gospels was rather strange. Four for him was a sacred number and corresponded to the four zones of the world, four principal winds, the four-faced cherubim in Ezekiel, and the living creatures in John's Revelation.[8] One could get the notion that he was reading from Philo or a Gnostic about a sacred number.

What was the position of the centralized church of the latter half of the second century concerning the epistles of Paul? Marcion had already

made ten of his epistles the major part of his canon. The freedom that
Paul declared and the liberty he gave to the churches he established were
incompatible with the highly developed ecclesiastical centralization of
this period. His democratic spirit was a threat to the hierarchy. As in his
own day when he had to defend his apostleship, so now the question was
raised: "Where did he get his authority as an apostle?" To be sure he was
not one of the Twelve. He had not been taught and commissioned by
Christ. Was Paul ordained? Was Paul in the apostolic succession?

Obviously, Irenaeus and Tertullian would have gladly obliterated the
epistles of Paul if they had not been so firmly fixed in the tradition.
Then, too, the popularity of Marcion in Christendom was so widespread
that any attempt by Irenaeus and Tertullian would have been met with
fierce resistance. How could the Church prove that Paul was subservient
to the apostolic college in Jerusalem? To Irenaeus and Tertullian the answer was simple. They would appeal to a document that—in their
minds—demonstrated this subordination. The document was the Acts of
the Apostles.

Previously in the writings of the Church Fathers there had been only
two or three uncertain quotations from this writing. Now it became the
chief book of the New Testament to legitimize Paul. Irenaeus and Tertullian reminded Marcion that Paul went to Jerusalem, and that there he
received his authority from the apostolic college. He was ordained and
received his apostolic succession. The Acts of the Apostles does not
teach this at all. After Peter went to the house of Cornelius at Caesarea,
he was downgraded as the leader of the church in Jerusalem and was re-
placed by James, the brother of Jesus, who was not one of the Twelve.
What would they do with Stephen, who was not one of the Twelve? He
was not in the apostolic succession, yet had it not been for his kind of
preaching, primitive Christianity might have ended up as a Galilean sect.

In addition to using the Acts of the Apostles to legitimize Paul, Irenaeus and Tertullian took the resounding declaration of independence by
Paul in Galatians 2 and completely changed it. Paul and Barnabas went
to Jerusalem and took with them Titus, who had not been circumcised
because he was a Greek. In a private session with Peter, James, and John,
Paul explained the freedom of the gospel that he preached among the
Gentiles. Then some false brothers were brought in who sought to spy
out the freedom of Paul and Barnabas and tried to suppress their evange-
listic efforts. But Paul said, "To them we did not yield in submission

even for a moment, in order that the truth of the gospel might be preserved for you" (Gal 2:15). Irenaeus and Tertullian said that the text had been altered by the insertion of a negative in the statement. Thus the reading should be, "For an hour I gave place by subjection." By the omission of a mere "not," Paul was transformed from a free man in Christ into a submissive believer in apostolic succession. How could they ignore the declaration of Paul in the very first verse of the letter to the Galatians that said, "Paul an Apostle not from men nor through a man, but through Jesus Christ and God the Father, who raised him from the dead." Or how could they ignore Paul's reprimand of Peter at Antioch when he refused to continue to eat with the Gentiles after the delegation from James arrived (2:14f). If Paul was not one of the Twelve but was subservient to the Twelve, how could he call Peter a hypocrite?

Irenaeus did not give a list of books that he considered to be a canon of the New Testament, but we have noticed that he did limit the Gospels to four. He also accepted Paul's epistles after he had made Paul subordinate to the Twelve. Irenaeus quoted from all of Paul's epistles including the Pastorals (1 Timothy, 2 Timothy, Titus), but he did not use Philemon. Irenaeus quoted copiously from the Acts of the Apostles, the document he employed to uphold the legitimacy of Paul. In one chapter of his work *Against Heresies*, of thirty-five quotations from the New Testament thirty are from the book of Acts. He used 1 John, 1 Peter, and Revelation but included no citations from Hebrews, Jude, 2 Peter, 2 and 3 John, and James. Strangely enough, Irenaeus received the *Shepherd of Hermas* as scripture,[9] and this was further confirmed by Eusebius.[10]

Tertullian did not enumerate the contents of the New Testament (*instrumentum*), but he did make comments about Jude and Hebrews. He accepted the epistle of Jude because 1 Enoch is quoted in it.[11] He was disturbed that 1 Enoch had been left out of the Old *Instrumentum* (the Old Testament). Apparently he did not know, as Clement of Alexandria tells us later, that Jude also quotes from the *Assumption of Moses*. Tertullian believed that Barnabas wrote the epistle to the Hebrews, but he felt that he had no authority to add it to the collection of sacred documents. He did say that he would accept Hebrews over the adulterous gospel of the *Shepherd of Hermas*. What was the problem? He and Irenaeus both accepted the doctrine of apostolic succession and the apostolic stand for the acceptance of sacred documents. In the Acts of the Apostles Barnabas is named an apostle just as was Paul. Since Tertullian was silent about

James, 2 Peter, and 2 and 3 John, we assume that he was not acquainted with these writings.

At some time in his career Tertullian became a Montanist. The Montanism that he accepted was a modified form prevalent in the West with some of the wild ideas of the East removed. He was probably enticed by the high moral and ethical principles of the Montanists. This, however, brought about a conflict of interest for the Carthaginian presbyter. How could he accept a closed period of revelation and at the same time support a Montanist doctrine of the continuation of the prophetic gift? How could he advocate apostolic succession and submission to the hierarchy, and at the same time uphold the teachings of the Montanists?

Tertullian said in his work, *Concerning Monogamy* 14: "For if Christ abrogated what Moses enjoined, because from the beginning it was so, why may not the Paraclete (Holy Spirit) abrogate an injunction which Paul granted?" When he opposed Marcion he said that the more ancient authority was the rule. In his work, *On the Veiling of Virgins* 1, he abandoned this principle completely and affirmed, "Whatever savors of opposition to truth will be heresy even if be an ancient custom. Christ is surnamed truth not tradition." What becomes of a final deposit of sacred writings if it is subject to modern prophets for alteration? Tertullian's puritanic way of life was tried exceedingly by the looseness of life in the church. Thus he said that the church is the Spirit, and its authority is that of the Spirit and not the number of bishops or presbyters (*Modesty* 21). He remained in the orthodox ecclesiastical system, but he also advocated the Montanist claim of a continuing revelation.

In the second century an attack was launched against the Montanists in Asia Minor, and in the early part of the third century a similar reaction occurred in Rome. In Asia Minor these opponents were labelled *Alogi* ("not logical") by Epiphanius, the bishop of Constantia (Salamis), in A.D. 375. Previous to that time they had not been given a name. Did the designator mean "senseless," "irrational," or those against the "logos" doctrine associated with the prologue of the Gospel of John? A decade or two later the Roman presbyter Gaius adopted the same position as that of the *Alogi*.

In response to the Montanists—who considered their leader as the new Paraclete (John 14:26, etc.) and anticipated the imminent descent of the new Jerusalem in Phrygia—the *Alogi* said that the Gospel of John and the book of Revelation were written by the Jewish-Christian heretic

Cerinthus. The *Alogi* might also have been levelling their guns of opposition at the Gnostics. We know that the Gnostics—in particular Valentinus, Heracleon, and Ptolemaus—were the ones who rescued the Gospel of John from obscurity and used it in their system of speculation. The remedy of the *Alogi* was uncritical. They tried to find unity for the church by removing the foundation for the Montanist dreamers and Gnostic philosophers.

The reaction to the Gospel of John and Revelation does not appear to have been an organized endeavor, but rather the opinion of a group of Christians who knew that something was wrong with the interpretations of the Gnostics and the Montanists; yet, they did not know how to handle the problem in any other manner than to reject these documents. Notably, the *Alogi* were never classed as heretics. They remained in the church because at that period of time criticism of the documents was tolerated when one opposed the heretics with the most drastic measures. Contrary to the *Alogi*, Irenaeus chose to accept the Gospel of John and claimed that the Gnostics who were not in the apostolic succession had no right to be interpreters of this Gospel.

The Muratorian Canon

In 1740 at the Ambrosian Library in Milan, Italy, an Italian archaeologist—Antonio Muratori—discovered the fragment of a manuscript that listed the books of the New Testament with attendant comments. It dates from the seventh or eighth century, but the text of the manuscript probably goes back as early as A.D. 180. Likely, the full copy contained a list of the Old Testament books. Unfortunately, the manuscript is mutilated at the beginning and the end. The author is unknown. Some scholars have suggested that Hegesippus, Hippolatus, or Papias wrote the document. An indication of the date of the fragment is found in lines 73 through 77 with these words about the *Shepherd of Hermas*: "The Shepherd was written quite recently in our times, while his brother Pius occupied the bishop's chair in the church of the city of Rome." (Pius was bishop from A.D. 139–154.) The fragment is written in crude Latin. Some suggest that it was originally written in Greek. If so, this might give some reason for the poor Latin translation by one skilled in Greek but unrefined in Latin. In the event that the fragment was written in Rome as early as A.D. 180, we assume that the original manuscript was in Greek, because Greek continued to be the Christian literary language into the third century.

The Muratorian Fragment was undoubtedly an attempt by someone in authority in the Roman Church to close the canon of Christian literature. Despite its brevity (only eighty-five lines), this writing gives a vast amount of information relative to the status of the New Testament along with criteria for the evaluation of the books. In the list of Gospels, Matthew and Mark do not occur because the manuscript is mutilated at the beginning. The ending of Mark is preserved, we assume, with this sentence, "At these, however, he was present and so he set them down." This assumption is based on the line that follows: "The third book of the Gospel according to Luke."

The author said that Luke was not an eyewitness or a hearer of Christ, but that he was Paul's travel companion. Through Luke's association with Paul, he was able to get the oral tradition that shaped his Gospel. Thus, the author quickly answered the question that someone might put to him, "By what authority did Luke compose his Gospel?" The answer is apostolic authority through Paul. If we had his comments about the Gospel of Mark, he probably would be in agreement with Papias and Irenaeus, who said that Mark was the interpreter of Peter. It seems that the apostolic standard prevails throughout the fragment.

The author gave special attention to John's Gospel. Only seven lines are devoted to Luke's Gospel, while twenty-five lines are given to John. This is a clear indication that he found it necessary to defend this Gospel. Perhaps he had in mind the *Alogi* who rejected the Gospel of John, as we have previously discussed. He gave a tale, which seems to be pure invention, about how John was persuaded to write. His fellow-disciples and bishops encouraged him to compose a Gospel, and his reply was, "Fast along with me three days from today, and whatever may be revealed to each, let us relate it to one another." On that very night it was revealed to the Apostle Andrew that John should write down everything in his own name, and that he and the fellow-disciples would make revisions. Apparently the author was trying to overcome the problem of John 21:24 ("We know that his testimony is true") by showing that disciples other than John were involved in the composition of the Gospel.

The author admitted in the fragment to differences in expression with the other Gospels, but he argued that there is no difference in faith since everything has been declared by one primary Spirit. The compilation of

John, Andrew, and other disciples owes its difference to revelation. Later, Clement of Alexandria noticed the difference between John and the other Gospels and contended that the other Gospels are corporeal; but John, at the instigation of his friends and by revelation, created a spiritual Gospel. Thus, Clement agreed with the Muratorian canon.

In the conclusion of his comments on John's Gospel, the author probably took a shot at the Gnostics who had a particular interest in this Gospel. He stressed the eyewitness character of John's account by quoting from 1 John 1:1-3, which affirms that he was not only a spectator but a hearer. Some scholars believe that he was not merely pointing out the personal association of John with Jesus, but setting up a contrast between the words of 1 John 1:1-3 and the Gnostics use of 1 Corinthians 2:9: "What no eye has seen, nor ear heard. . . ." The source of the quotation by Paul is unknown, but in the Gnostic works of the *Gospel of Thomas* (v. 17) and the *Acts of Peter* (v. 39), the words are attributed to Jesus. Some of the Gnostic circles used this quotation to promise their initiates that they would experience the deep mysteries of Christianity in which the common people could not share.

Following his comments on John, the author made an exaggerated declaration about the book of Acts. He said that Luke wrote "the Acts of all the Apostles." What a tremendous document that would have been! The only activity of the apostles in the book is that of Peter, John, and Paul. The fragment also claims that Luke had personal knowledge of all the details that he recorded. Again, this is an overstatement of the case. The author agreed that Luke omits Peter's death and Paul's journey to Spain. Why did he say this? The apocryphal *Acts of Peter* begins with Paul's trip to Spain from Ostia and ends with the crucifixion of Peter in Rome. Could it be that the author of the fragment was upholding the authenticity of one book of Acts in opposition to the five apocryphal Acts?

The list continues and refers to Paul's epistles. Contrary to Marcion, the author included the pastorals—making a total of thirteen. Exclusive of the pastorals and Philemon, however, he affirmed that the apostle wrote to seven churches. In the enumeration of seven churches he attempted to make Paul's writings conform to the pattern of John in Revelation. In this he was mistaken because Paul wrote to several churches in Galatia. Then, too, how could Paul have followed the precedent set by John when his letters were written before Revelation? What was the compiler trying to prove? Since Revelation is the only document in the

New Testament that in itself claims to be a revelation (Rev 1:1), the author appeared to be introducing another criterion of canonicity, that of prophetic inspiration. If so, then this standard for him was more significant than apostolicity. Only later did Clement of Alexandria use inspiration as a criterion for inclusion of books in the New Testament.

We also detect another criterion for canonicity in the symbolism of the number seven in Paul's epistles and the seven letters in Revelation. Seven is a complete number and demonstrates the universality of the message in the epistles. Paul would be amazed to learn that what he wrote to churches was so general in nature. He wrote to individual churches that were overwhelmed by all sorts of problems, controversies, misunderstandings, and pagan practices. He had no notion that he was writing for all churches of all times. In fact he would be surprised to know that his letters ultimately became scripture.

The author of the fragment realized that some of Paul's letters were sent to individuals—Timothy, Titus, and Philemon. How can letters sent to individuals be universal in scope? The author insisted that they had been hallowed for the honor of the Catholic Church in the regulation of ecclesiastical discipline.

The compiler went on to say that Jude and two of John's epistles (probably 1 and 2 John) were accepted in the Catholic Church. Two Revelations were known by the writer: the Revelation of John and the Revelation of Peter. He said that some would not allow the Revelation of Peter to be read in church. He omitted 1 and 2 Peter, James, Hebrews, and one epistle of John. It is not surprising that he left out Hebrews because Tertullian rejected it, since he thought it was written by Barnabas. What is amazing to us is his omission of 1 Peter, because this book was well established in the Roman church. Again we are astonished that he placed the apocryphal Old Testament book, the Wisdom of Solomon, in the New Testament list. With respect to the *Shepherd of Hermas*, he stated that it could be read (presumably in private) but could not be given to the people in the church. Apparently he set forth a fourth criterion for the acceptance of New Testament books: the standard of antiquity. The writing must fall within a given period of time, and the lateness of the date of the Shepherd disqualifies its acceptance.

The fragment rejects letters forged in the name of Paul (the letters to the Laodiceans and Alexandrines) and accuses the Marconites of the forgery. Also rejected are the writings of Arsinous, Valentinus, Miltiades, and a book of Marcionite psalms.

The Muratorian fragment must have been composed by one in authority, a bishop or an honored presbyter. It was probably written to those who were uncertain about the new collection of sacred literature. While the author may have been one who had authority, we have no indication that he was introducing a novel theory about the New Testament books. He spoke throughout the writing of a received and general opinion without risking an individual judgment. His appeal was to the Catholic Church, and this leads one to believe that it was in tune with the pulse-beat of Rome.

Notes

[1]Eusebius, *Ecclesiastical History* 3.39.4.
[2]Justin Martyr, *Apology* 1.67.
[3]Irenaeus, *Against Heresies* 3.11.9.
[4]Tertullian, *Against Marcion* 4.2.
[5]Eusebius, 3.39.15.
[6]Ibid., 3.39.16.
[7]Irenaeus, 3.1.1.
[8]*Ibid.*, 3.11.8.
[9]*Ibid.*, 4.20.2.
[10]Eusebius, 5.8.7.
[11]Tertullian, *On Women's Dress* 1.2.3.

Chapter Three

Soundings from the Eastern Churches

Heretofore we have taken soundings on the formation of the New Testament in Western churches, but now is the time to explore the opinions of the Eastern churches. By Western churches I mean those where the Latin language was spoken such as in Gaul, Italy, and North Africa. In the Eastern churches Greek and Syriac were the predominant languages. The churches of this character were found in Greece, Egypt, Asia Minor, Syria, Palestine, and Assyria. At this juncture we turn toward Alexandria in Egypt because it was the most significant center for the finalizing of the New Testament. Here we are in the company of Pantaenus, Clement, Origen, Dionysius, and Athanasius.

In Alexandria three religio-cultural trends came in succession from the time of the founding of the city in 332 B.C. until the establishment of a catechetical school under Pantaenus and continued by his successors. These trends touch directly or indirectly on the canon of the New Testament. The first religio-cultural trend was associated with the university of Hellenistic culture that flourished in the Museum and libraries of Alexandria. In the early days of the Museum, scholars were more concerned about literary works. They concentrated on textual and philological research aimed at establishing reliable critical texts of Greek manuscripts. Their investigations included textual criticism, grammar, interpretation, syntactical study, and literary criticism. Scribes were employed under royal patronage to copy classical masterpieces. Others compiled lexicons and grammars based on the work of Dionysius Thrax of Rhodes, who flourished about 100 B.C. In a short time Alexandria became a rendezvous for adherents of the various forms of Greek philosophy.

Later, the interests of the scholars in the Museum shifted to pursuits in the scientific field. This new dimension of inquiry, plus the achievements of the textual and literary critics, pushed the city into the forefront as the intellectual center of the world. The particular scientific interests were mathematics, anatomy, astronomy, zoology, botany, medicine, physiology, and geography.

A second religio-cultural tendency in Alexandria was the Judeo-Alexandrian school of thought. The Jews had formed an ethnic group in the city from the time of Ptolemy I. They could not isolate themselves in language, economics, and culture from the other inhabitants. The Jews adopted the Greek Koine (common Greek) as the language of their everyday conversation, and under Ptolemy Philadelphus translated the Old Testament (at least the Pentateuch) from the Hebrew language into Greek. This translation, known as the *Septuagint*, was a great monument for Judaism in the Dispersion. The Jews in Alexandria took advantage of the abundance of classical and Hellenistic writings in the library and produced the largest collection of Jewish-Hellenistic literature in existence. Most of the literature was a defense of Judaism against the criticisms of Gentiles and a presentation of their religion and way of life to Gentile God-fearers.

The most illustrious Jewish scholar in Alexandria was Philo (19 B.C. –49 A.D.). His extremely wealthy brother, Alexander, was the Alabarch (political head of the Jewish community of Alexandria). Philo attempted to combine Greek thought and learning with Jewish religion. In his writings he named over sixty-four Greek writers and frequently referred to Homer, Hesiod, Pindar, Solon, the Greek tragedians, Plato, and others. He pointed out, however, that Moses was greater than all the Greek thinkers, including Plato. He believed that all the philosophers had borrowed their systems from Moses, in whom all truth was found.

Philo accepted a method of interpretation that already was used by the Stoics to give meaning to literature and remove its immoral and barbarous elements. This method was the allegory. The Stoics believed that words were veils of hidden meanings. When Philo adopted their idea, the most trivial incidents in the Bible contained for him deep metaphysical truths. Whenever a literal interpretation might imply some idea or fact unworthy of God or contrary to reason, Philo turned to allegory. Early Christian writers were pleased with this method, but while Philo's interests in allegory were limited to the Pentateuch, the Alexandrian fathers of the Christian faith, as well as some in the Western churches, focused their attention on the prophets and poetry of the Old Testament and the teachings of Jesus in the New Testament.

The third religio-cultural trend in Alexandria was the Christian cate-chetical school. The school of Christian teaching in the city was more famous and significant than the earlier Greek and Jewish schools. According to legend, Mark was the founder of the school. The first evidence for the existence of the institution, however, names Pantaenus as the orig-inator. Pantaenus, a Stoic philosopher, organized the "school of the faithful" after he was converted to Christianity about A.D. 185. Prior to this time, the Christians of Alexandria apparently were given instruction in the faith by bishops, presbyters, and deacons by means of private les-sons. Those who desired a higher education went to the public rhetorical school and the university.

Christian education in rhetoric and philosophy became important for two reasons. Gnosticism had made itself known in Alexandria through Basilides, his son Isodore, and others; and this type of religious philos-ophy was corrupting the Church. Another reason for this school was that Christianity was gaining a new constituency. The frequent conversion of the educated pagans, even scholars and philosophers, made it necessary for the bishop to entrust the instruction of these learners to the scholarly educated Christians.

After Pantaenus, Clement (not the Clement of Rome) became head of the school. He, like Justin Martyr and Tatian, had studied under phil-osophers from Greece, Syria, Palestine, Assyria, and southern Italy. He probably was an Athenian by birth. Finally he became a student of Panta-enus about the year A.D. 190. His literary activity seems to have been between A.D. 190–202. Clement was head of the school until A.D. 202 when he fled from Alexandria to Cappadocia in order to escape the per-secution under Severus. He was a presbyter in the Alexandrian church, the teacher of Origen, and the father of Greek theology. At the age of eighteen, Origen was appointed by Bishop Demetrius the successor of Clement as head of the school. From A.D. 202–231 he flourished in this position and became known as the greatest scholar of the ancient church. His fame as a biblical scholar in the areas of textual criticism and inter-pretation, plus the reputation as the first systematic theologian, attracted distinguished scholars and even heretics from all parts of the world. Many of his twenty-nine years as head of the school were spent in exile due to persecutions in Alexandria by Roman emperors. In A.D. 231 Origen was banished from Alexandria by Bishop Demetrius. He then went to Caesarea Maritima in Palestine, where he established another school after the pattern of the one in Alexandria.

The directors of the Alexandrian school after Origen were Heraclas, Dionysius, Theognostus, Pierius, and Peter, but none of these rose to the height of their predecessors. During the fourth century the institution passed more and more into obscurity, probably because of the lack of famous teachers, the domination of church authorities like Athanasius, and the fanaticism of ignorant monks. The theology on which the studies of the Alexandrian school were based was influenced tremendously by Plato and the allegorical method of interpretation. It was replete with errors but very influential in Christendom, both then and now.

Pantaenus and Clement

We know very little about Pantaenus and his teachings. If the "blessed presbyter" quoted by Eusebius from Clement's *Hypotyposes* (Outlines) was Pantaenus, then he was the first person to declare that Paul wrote Hebrews.[1] His explanation for Paul's name not being associated with the epistle is very naive. Since Paul was an apostle to the Gentiles, out of modesty he did not inscribe himself as an apostle to the Hebrews. This view is in opposition to Tertullian, who said that the epistle was written by Barnabas.

Tertullian had asked, "What has Athens to do with Jerusalem?"[2] The reply of Clement would have been similar to that of Justin before him. For him Plato was divinely inspired. In the philosophy of Plato, Clement discovered the foreshadowing of Christian teaching. It appears that Clement, like Philo, was swayed by the Greek concept of inspiration tied in with oracular utterances and mystical experiences rather than the Hebrew notion of a personal encounter with God. He was probably influenced by Philo in pressing for the inspiration of the Septuagint version of the Old Testament.

Clement said that those Gospels that contain the genealogies (Matthew and Luke) were written first. About Mark he followed essentially the tradition of Papias with this exception. He declared that those who were present with Mark insisted on his writing a gospel. Clement did not give the story of how John came to write a gospel, as did the Muratorian canon, though he did note that John was exhorted by his friends to compose a work.

> But John last of all, aware that the bodily facts had been set forth in (other) Ggospels, yielded to the exhortation of his friends and, divinely carried by the Spirit, composed a spiritual Gospel.[3]

In a literary composition called *Stromata* he quotes from the *Gospel of the Egyptians* four times. Admittedly he did not recognize it as being on a par with the four Gospels, but he had no sharp feeling of uneasiness about using it. This might also be said about his use of the *Gospel of the Hebrews* and the esoteric treatise known as the *Traditions of Matthias*.

Clement clearly recognized the book of Acts as scripture and repeatedly affirmed that it was a work of Luke. He accepted all of Paul's epistles, including the epistle to the Hebrews, but his theory about the epistle was not the same as that of Pantaenus. He believed that Paul wrote the letter in Hebrew and Luke published it in Greek for the benefit of Greek-speaking readers.

In one of the extracts from Clement's lost *Hypotyposes*, Eusebius said that Clement gave "short comments on all testamented scripture not passing by the books that are spoken against, I mean the epistle of Jude and the rest of the Catholic epistles, and both Barnabas and the Revelation called Peter's."[4] According to Cassiodorus of Calabria (sixth century), who wrote a handbook for monks, the Catholic epistles commented on in *Hypotyposes* were 1 Peter, 1 and 2 John and James. James was probably a mistake by some copyist and it should read "Jude." Likely, Clement did not comment on 2 Peter, James, or 3 John. He did not hesitate to use the Revelation of John. [5]

Clement introduced the criterion of inspiration for the inclusion of documents in the New Testament. This standard had been implied in the Muratorian canon but was made more explicit by Clement. Clement's use of this criterion allowed him to incorporate documents that no one would accept today. By citing them as scripture or appealing to them in an authoritative manner, he accepted a wider range of books than was agreed to by other churches in the East and West, namely: the *Revelation of Peter*, *1 Clement*, the *Preaching of Peter*, the *Didache*, and the *Shepherd of Hermas*.

Clement's Old Testament was the Septuagint (a Greek translation) that he, like Philo, believed to be inspired of God. It included the apocryphal works that were rejected by the Jews. In addition, he used other non-canonical Jewish documents, namely: the Assumption of Moses, 1 Enoch, and the Revelation of Zephaniah. Only through Clement do we learn that Jude used the Assumption of Moses in verse 9.[6]

Origen

When Clement left Alexandria during the persecution of Severus, Origen became his successor as director of the catechetical school. From the hardships and sufferings that he endured during his early years and even throughout his career, we would never have thought that he could have achieved such prominence in ecclesiastical history. He was born in Alexandria about A.D. 185 and died about A.D. 254 in Caesarea or Tyre. His father, Leonides, was put to death in the persecution under Serverus in A.D. 202. At an early age he enjoyed the catechetical instructions of Clement. After the death of his father, Origen, his mother, and six smaller brothers were left destitute because all of his father's property was confiscated. A certain rich lady—probably because she saw the potential in Origen—took him into her household. She had previously adopted a son named Paul of Antioch. Because Origen considered Paul a heretic, he later left the household and taught grammar in the city. Bishop Demetrius heard about the ability of Origen to attract pagans through his teaching and named him the new director of the catechetical school vacated by Clement.

In A.D. 228 Origen took a trip to Greece and on the way allowed himself to be ordained a presbyter by the bishops of Jerusalem and Caesarea. Demetrius was opposed because he contended that Origen was unworthy of the presbyter's office since he had emasculated himself, and, furthermore, he had not asked for Demetrius' consent. The matter was put to rest, and Origen was reconciled to Demetrius. He returned to Alexandria, but for some unknown reason a new dissension arose between Origen and Demetrius. Origen left Alexandria for Caesarea in A.D. 231. In his absence Demetrius accused him before the council of erroneous ideas in matters of the Christian faith. The majority approved of the accusations of Demetrius, and Origen was defrocked as presbyter.

Origen's testimony concerning the Old Testament and the New Testament is of exceptional value because the information is not localized. He knew of the traditions in Rome, Antioch, Athens, and Caesarea by his visits to those cities during persecutions in Alexandria. He opened lines of communication with those churches that proved to be advantageous to him and to his successor Dionysius. Upon the basis of his personal knowledge of the existing use of New Testament documents in various ecclesiastical provinces of his day, he cautiously made his own judgments relative to the value of each writing. Quite frequently one will find some vacillation and inconsistency in his opinions, but this tendency on his part may be explained by his gaining further knowledge in his travels and his final stay in Caesarea after his banishment.

In his commentary on Psalm 1, Origen gave a list (preserved by Eusebius) of the Old Testament books, with their Hebrew and Greek names.[7] Unfortunately this list excludes the Twelve prophets and includes the apocryphal Epistle of Jeremiah, which is joined with Jeremiah and Lamentations. The omission of what we know as the Minor Prophets probably came through transmission either by Origen or Eusebius, and the inclusion of the Epistle of Jeremiah may have been a careless mistake. By "careless mistake" I do not wish to imply that Origen was opposed to using the Apocrypha as part of the Old Testament. Apparently, his list was intended to conform to the limits prescribed by the Christians in Caesarea and the Palestinian Jews.

Before he went to Caesarea, Origen freely used the Septuagint (the Christian Greek translation of the Old Testament that included the Apocrypha). He believed that whatever was in the Septuagint should be used by Christians. In addition to the Apocrypha he was acquainted with other apocryphal writings, namely: the Assumption of Moses, the Apocalypse of Elijah, the Ascension of Isaiah, and the Testaments of the Twelve Patriarchs. At one time he accepted 1 Enoch but later doubted its authority.

As a textual critic of the Old Testament, Origen's most important work was the *Hexapla*. This was a compilation of texts presented side by side in six vertical columns. In sequence the columns represented the Hebrew text, the Hebrew text in Greek, Aquila's Greek version, Symmachus' Greek version, the Septuagint used by Origen, and Theodotion's Greek version. Aquila, Symmachus, and Theodotion were Jews of the second century A.D. who made translations of the Hebrew scripture into Greek to offset the official Greek translation of the Christians. The fifth column contained Origen's edition of the Septuagint, and this edition had a considerable influence on the text in subsequent ages. Seeing that there were conflicting versions of the Old Testament, he determined to bring them together and use them to produce a more accurate version.

The most significant characteristic of Origen's work on the canon was his appeal to ecclesiastical recognition. His decision about the books was based on church usage. This led him to make a distinction with respect to the various writings. Among the acknowledged books he listed were the four Gospels, Acts, the Pauline epistles, 1 Peter, 1 John, and Revelation. His disputed books were 2 Peter, 2 and 3 John, Hebrews, James, and Jude. A third classification was the false writings. The Gospels of the Egyptians, Thomas, Basilides, and Matthias he rejected as heretical forgeries.

Most of our knowledge of Origen's position on the New Testament comes from Eusebius, who collected quotations from Origen's commentary on Matthew, an exposition of John, and sermons on Hebrews. He was the first Christian writer to mention 2 Peter. He said, "Peter again, on whom the church of Christ is built against which the gates of hell shall not prevail, has left behind one epistle generally acknowledged; perhaps also a second, for it is a disputed question."[8] Concerning the epistles of John, Origen remarked, "(John) has left behind also one epistle of very few lines: perhaps too a second and third; for all do not allow that these are genuine."[9] In his *Homilies* on the epistle to the Hebrews, he gave a rather lengthy discussion of authorship. He drew attention to the difference in style between Paul's epistles and that of Hebrews, but quickly noted that the thoughts were not inferior to those of acknowledged apostolical writings. Therefore, he concluded that the thoughts were of Paul, but the document was composed by one who took notes on the teaching of the apostle. If any church said that Paul wrote it, he agreed that that was all right. But then he added, "Who wrote the epistle, the truth God knows." Through tradition he learned that some believed Clement of Rome was the author while others held that Luke wrote it.[10]

Origen quoted from Hebrews more than 200 times, introducing the quotation with the Apostle, the epistle to the Hebrews, or Paul, or Paul in the epistle to the Hebrews. Concerning Jude, he wrote in his commentary on Matthew 13:55 that the epistle was written by Jude, the brother of Jesus. In the same comment he identified James as the Lord's brother, but he did not refer to the epistle of James. Later on in the commentary he indicated that the epistle of Jude was not acknowledged by all the churches. In the fifth century Rufinus made a Latin translation of Origen's *Homilies* on Genesis and Joshua, and in them we discover two passages in which he enumerated the different authors of books of the New Testament. The first passage is from Genesis 13:2, where he gave a spiritual explanation concerning the wells that Isaac reopened after the Philistines had filled them up. The new wells dug by Isaac are spiritually interpreted, so that all authors of the New Testament were given the role of servants of Isaac in digging new wells, even James and Jude.

The second passage is found in Origen's *Homilies on Joshua*. In the sermon on Joshua 7:1 again he spiritualized the blasts from the trumpets of the priests that produced the crumbling of the walls of Jericho as he had spiritualized the wells in Genesis to list the authors of the New Testament. He spoke of the twofold trumpet of Peter's epistles, of Jude and of James. He also joined Hebrews with the other thirteen of Paul's epistles to make fourteen trumpets.

In the passages above we are not willing to accept fully the lists that are given because we are aware that Rufinius, in his Latin translation, was quite frequently guilty of harmonizing Origen with current belief. Then, too, we might add that Origen's sermons were for spiritual instruction rather than critical inquiry.

Unlike his predecessor Clement, Origen had doubts about the *Preaching of Peter*, but he did acknowledge *Barnabas*, the *Didache*, and the *Shepherd of Hermas* as Scripture. Origen knew the epistle of Clement; however, there is no indication that he considered it as scripture. Robert Grant has contended that Origen accepted *Barnabas*, the *Didache*, and the *Shepherd of Hermas* while he resided in Alexandria, but when he went to Caesarea, he discovered these documents were not received there.[11]

In an Alexandrian setting where precedents had been established by Philo and the Gnostics who discerned deep spiritual truths and mysteries in the most simple teachings, Clement and his successor Origen could with integrity accept both canonical and non-canonical writings as long as they were confident that these writings contained, on the basis of allegorical interpretation, spiritual meanings.

Dionysius

After Origen left Alexandria in A.D. 231 and went to Caesarea, Dionysius—one of Origen's most distinguished students—was appointed
head of the catechetical school and in A.D. 247 was named bishop of
Alexandria. In the course of his career Dionysius maintained intimate
communication with Rome, Asia Minor, and Palestine. Fragments of his
letters, preserved by Eusebius, contain numerous references to the New
Testament. His most important contribution to the study of the New Testament canon was his thorough discussion of Revelation. Until his time
there had been no critical examination of the document.

Dionysius, using evidence based on language, style, and contents, declared that Revelation could not stem from the author of the Gospel or
1 John.[12] He said that some before him had cast aside the book, saying
that it was written by Cerinthus who forged the name of John to give cre-
dence to his own fabrication. He admitted that he had nothing against the
writer of Revelation being called John and agreed that the author was
inspired and holy, but he refused to believe that John—the apostle and
son of Zebedee—wrote it. Dionysius did not reject Revelation, but he did
raise the question of its apostolicity. In this he possibly implied that the
book was not on the same level with those books that had gained recognition in the church due to their apostolic nature. It might just be that he
turned the Gospel and 1 John against Revelation, as Robert Grant suggested, "in order to diminish the apocalyptic fervor of Egyptian monks
in his diocese."[13]

Eusebius

When Origen went to Caesarea in A.D. 231, he established a school on
the pattern of the one in Alexandria. Likely he did much to enlarge the
library there, and quite possibly the library contained his own books. We
have no knowledge of the school and library after the death of Origen
until the time of Pamphilus, a native of Berytus in Phoenicia (now Beirut
in Lebanon). Pamphilus studied at Alexandria under Pierius, a student of
Origen, and became a presbyter at Caesarea under Bishop Agapius. Tradition has it that he founded the library at Caesarea, but it is more likely

that his extraordinary care of the library can account for its being called "the library of the holy Pamphilus." As a great admirer of Origen, he got involved in the Origenistic controversy. Pamphilus and Eusebius of Caesarea were so closely associated with each other that the latter took the name of the former and was called Eusebius Pamphilus. They combined to write an *Apology for Origen*. We can readily see that the voice of Caesarea on the canon is essentially that of the Alexandrian scholars.

Eusebius has been called the Father of Church History. Between A.D. 305–325 he composed his *Ecclesiastical History,* which contains a large part of our knowledge of the first three centuries of Christianity. As a historian he did not possess the historiographer's skill of criticism of details, nor did he record the proper sequence of events. Nevertheless, had it not been for his diligence in utilizing the materials that he possessed, they would have been lost. His history is invaluable to us as a repository of useful facts and documents.

In A.D. 313 Eusebius became bishop of Caesarea. During his episcopate the Arian controversy arose; he took an intermediate position between Arius and Athanasius, based on the view of Origen. During the Council of Nicaea in A.D. 325, he tried to reconcile the two contending parties, but to no avail. His attempt at reconciliation, however, gained for him the friendship of Emperor Constantine. After writing his history, Constantine asked Eusebius to make fifty copies of both Testaments in Greek and defrayed the cost. The copies were to be made by trained scribes and written on good parchment. This put Eusebius in the position of having to incorporate books of the New Testament that were disputed in some churches.

Eusebius basically followed the Alexandrians in their opinions on New Testament books that were based on church usage. In chapter 25 of Book 3 he set forth four classifications of the Christian writings: the universally confessed or acknowledged books, those that were disputed, the spurious, and the rejected books. Under the acknowledged documents he listed the four Gospels, Acts, the epistles of Paul, 1 John, 1 Peter, and Revelation. As to Revelation, he gave a parenthetical remark "if it seemed proper." He did not enumerate the epistles of Paul, but he must have included Hebrews because it is not listed in the disputed books. Previously he had said that Hebrews was disputed by the church in Rome as not being by Paul (3.3.4f), but he decided to accept it as Pauline on the basis of the Alexandrian tradition.

In the second category he listed the disputed books, but he knew that these were recognized by the majority of churches. He named the epistles of James and Jude, 2 Peter, "and the so-called second and third epistles of John, whether these are by the evangelist or by someone else with the same name."

In the spurious division of documents he placed the *Acts of Paul*, the *Shepherd of Hermas*, the *Apocalypse of Peter*, the *Epistle of Barnabas*, the *Teachings of the Apostles* (*Didache*), the *Gospel of Hebrews*, and *Revelation*. Eusebius had the same parenthetical remark about Revelation here as he had when he included the book among the acknowledged ones. Clearly, he did not know how to classify Revelation. He raised the question of where to place it—with the confessed books or with the spurious books? Perhaps his unsettled position on the writing was due to Dionysius' rejection of John, the apostle, as author.

A fourth classification by Eusebius had to do with books that were rejected. He refused them because they were written by heretics who pretended that the books were written by apostles. In this list he included the *Gospel of Peter*, the *Gospel of Thomas*, the *Gospel of Matthias*, the *Acts of Andrew, the Acts of John*, and other acts purportedly written by apostles. The two criteria for determining the rejection of books were the apostolic standard and true orthodoxy. The heretical works were"not even to be ranged among the spurious (books), but to be rejected as totally absurd and impious."

From the time when Eusebius completed his *Ecclesiastical History* about A.D. 325 until the Festal Epistle of Athanasius in A.D. 367, we encounter no more witnesses to the canon of the New Testament in the East. Some might ask, "What about the list in the sixtieth canon of the Council of Laodicea in A.D. 363?" Indeed, a catalogue of the Old Testament books exists that agrees with the Jewish canon plus the list of the twenty-six books of the New Testament with the omission of Revelation, but questions have been raised by scholars on the date of the council as well as the integrity of the sixtieth canon.

Athanasius

Athanasius, sometimes called the Father of Orthodoxy, could by no means measure up to the calibre of the Alexandrian scholars who preceded him. He was born in Alexandria and died in A.D. 373. He was a bitter opponent of Arius. At the Council of Nicaea in A.D. 325, a council summoned at the request of Emperor Constantine to deal with the Arian controversy, Athanasius showed strong feelings of emotion against Eusebius of Caesarea, who sought reconciliation with the Arians. The outcome of the council should have pleased him because the Nicaean Creed that was adopted embraced his orthodoxy. His resentment against the Arians reached an all-time high when Eusebius of Nicomedia insisted, possibly through an order by the emperor, that Arius be readmitted to the church. Athanasius' continued hostility resulted in his banishment four times during the reign of Constantine and his successor Constantinus.

When Alexander died in A.D. 328, Athanasius was appointed bishop of Alexandria. As a result of the Council of Nicaea in A.D. 325, the bishop of Alexandria was officially designated to send a letter to all Christendom indicating the date for the celebration of Easter. The probable reasoning behind this official duty was tied to the superior astronomical knowledge found in Alexandria. During his forty-five years as bishop, Athanasius wrote a festal letter each year making the announcement of the date of Easter, but along with the proclamation he included other important information. In his Thirty-ninth Festal Epistle of A.D. 367, he listed the books of the Old and New Testaments.

After patterning his introduction "to the place of the Gospel of Luke," which we call the preface, he gave a catalogue of the books of the Old Testament. He omitted Esther and joined the epistle of Jeremiah and Baruch, both apocryphal books, to the prophet Jeremiah and to Lamentations. In his New Testament canon we find all twenty-seven books with no doubts registered about any. In an authoritative and dictatorial manner he said: "These are the fountains of salvation, that they who thirst may be satisfied with the living words they contain. In these alone is proclaimed the teaching of godliness. No person is to add to these, neither can he take anything from these." The "add and take from" is probably lifted from Revelation 22:19.

Athanasius concluded the epistle by naming apocryphal books "not indeed included in the canon but appointed by the Fathers to be read by those who newly join us and who wish for instruction in the word of godliness." For the Old Testament apocryphal writings he listed the *Wisdom of Solomon*, *Jesus ben Sira*, *Esther*, *Judith*, and *Tobit*. For the New Testament apocryphal writings he included the *Didache* and the *Shepherd*

of Hermas. He dismissed other apocryphal works as inventions of heretics to lead the simple astray. Athanasius was the first person to call this
ecclesiastically fixed collection of Holy Scriptures the *canon*. (He used
the participle form of the verb *kanonizō* three times in the epistle.)

Had there been any further evidence advanced in the Eastern churches since A.D. 325 to justify Athanasius' removal of doubts about some of
the catholic epistles as well as Revelation? We know of none. Could it
be that he took advantage of his authority to declare when Easter was to
be observed by also defining the canon in order to deliver a blow to his
arch enemy, Eusebius of Caesarea, who wavered on some of the catholic
epistles and Revelation? This does not seem possible, though we must
admit he hated Eusebius with a passion.

Is it possible that during one of his banishments while in Rome Athanasius compared the opinions of the West with the East among the
officials in Rome and that some sort of an agreement was reached? In the
West there were doubts about Hebrews; and James, 2 Peter, and 3 John
were seemingly not known. 2 Peter, James, and 3 John were known but
disputed in the East. Jude was accepted in the West but in the East was
rejected because of doubts about it. Revelation was definitely in the canon in the East, but in the East, Dionysius and Eusebius both showed
some indecision concerning its acceptance. Until A.D. 397 at the Third
Council of Carthage, Hebrews never enjoyed canonicity in the West. It
was met with acceptance, however, by the scholars of Alexandria and Eusebius of Caesarea because Paul's name was associated with it. We can
conjecture that during his stay in Rome Athanasius worked out some sort
of compromise for the West and East.

We must bear in mind that no council of bishops and presbyters
cleared up the matter of the canon once and for all. The settlement came
solely on the authority of Athanasius, the bishop of Alexandria. Just as
Irenaeus and Tertullian were surrounded by a great cloud of heretics, so
was Athanasius. Just as Irenaeus and Tertullian ordered the heretics off
their territory and defined the reliable books for the Christian community
on the basis of the authority of apostolic succession, so Athanasius ended
the process of choosing books, canonized those he considered orthodox,
and left the heretics hanging helplessly with their imitation scriptures.

Athanasius and the Eastern Churches

What influence did Athanasius' catalogue of books of the Old Testament and the New Testament contained in his Thirty-ninth Festal epistle have upon the Eastern churches? We have no evidence to draw a conclusion, but we assume that they were not overpowered by his self-assured authority to determine the canon. Essentially there was agreement with the catalogue of Old Testament books, but doubts were still manifested concerning New Testament writings.

Cyril (A.D. 315–386), the bishop of Jerusalem, in one of his catechetical lectures, named all the books of the New Testament except Revelation. He probably wrote the lecture in A.D. 346, so his omission of the book would not show a reaction to Athanasius. Gregory of Nazianzus was in touch with traditions from other eastern churches. He studied in Caesarea of Cappadocia, Caesarea of Palestine, and in Athens for ten years. For a short time he was bishop of Constantinople. It is not known when he composed his metrical list of genuine books of the Old and New Testaments, but, interestingly enough, he left out Revelation. Amphilochius, a Cappadocian lawyer, became bishop of Iconium. In *Poem to Seleucus*, found among the poems of Gregory of Nazianzus and written about A.D. 380, he said that some declared Hebrews spurious, but he thought "its grace is genuine." As to the catholic epistles he mentioned that some received only three—James, 1 Peter, and 1 John— while others accepted all seven. He affirmed that the majority rejected Revelation, but some included it as genuine.

John Chrysostom was a prolific writer, preacher, and bishop of Constantinople from A.D. 397 to 407. If he had given a list of New Testament books, he would have reflected the usage of documents in the Syrian church, because he was born in Antioch in Syria. With the exception of a doubtful quotation from 2 Peter 2:22 (this could have come from Proverbs 26:11), nowhere did he refer to four of the catholic epistles (2 Peter, 2 and 3 John, and Jude) nor to Revelation.

Theodore of Mopsuestia, a priest in Antioch from A.D. 383 until his appointment as bishop of Mopsuestia in Cilicia in A.D. 392, was a very close friend of John Chrysostom. He was in today's terms a "historical critical exegete." He wrote commentaries on Matthew, Luke, and John, plus commentaries on the fourteen epistles of Paul. According to Leontius of Byzantium, who flourished in the sixth century, he rejected "the epistle of James and the other catholic epistles." Some think that the quotation of Leontius means that he rejected James, 2 and 3 John, and 2 Peter but accepted 1 Peter and 1 John. We could imagine that Theodore rejected all the catholic epistles. Nothing is known of his judgment on Revelation, but it is possible that he did omit it since he belonged to the school of Antioch.

Other evidence for the status of the Bible in the East comes from early manuscripts. Three uncial codices of the Greek Bible, copied in the fourth and fifth centuries A.D., show us what books were deemed worthy to be bound into a collection of sacred literature. Codex Sinaiticous, a fourth-century manuscript, was discovered by Tischendorf at St. Catherine's monastery at Mount Sinai. Much of the Old Testament has been lost, but the surviving Old Testament includes the apocryphal books of *Tobit, Judith, 1 and 4 Maccabees, Jesus ben Sira,* and the *Wisdom of Solomon.* It is the only early manuscript to preserve all the New Testament books with the complete text. To the New Testament were added the *Epistle of Barnabas* and the *Shepherd.* Codex Sinaiticus is now found in the British Museum in London.

Codex Vaticanus, another fourth-century manuscript, includes the apocryphal works of *Jesus ben Sira,* the *Wisdom of Solomon, Judith, Tobit,* and the *Epistle of Jeremiah* (the books of *Maccabees* are omitted as part of the Old Testament). We do not know all the books of the New Testament that were contained in the manuscript because the manuscript ends in the middle of Hebrews and the rest of the New Testament may have included the letters to Timothy, Titus, and Philemon, and the book of Revelation. This manuscript resides in the Vatican library in Rome.

The third uncial, Alexandrinus, is later in date than the two above. It comes from the first half of the fifth century. It too contains the Apocrypha as part of the Old Testament. In addition to what are found in the two uncials above, this manuscript adds *Baruch,* four books of *Maccabees,* and the *Psalms of Solomon.* The *Psalms of Solomon* is listed, but the text is not given. In the New Testament we note that 1 and 2 Clement were added after Revelation. The manuscript is placed next to Codex Sinaiticus in the British Museum.

In addition to the above manuscripts, we have a further early witness to the books of the New Testament affirmed to be authentic by the eastern churches. This is the translation of the Greek text into Syriac by Rabbula, the bishop of Edessa from A.D. 411–435. The version is known as the Peshitta. All copies of this translation omitted 2 Peter, 2 and 3 John, Jude, and Revelation. Later revisions of Peshitta accepted those books that were left out.

Notes

[1]Eusebius, *Ecclesiastical History*, 6.14.4.
[2]Tertullian, *Prescription of Heretics*, 7.
[3]Eusebius, 6.14.5-7.
[4]*Ibid.*, 6.14.1.
[5]Clement of Alexandria, *Stromata*, 6.13.
[6]Clement of Alexandria, *Adumbrationes on Jude.*
[7]Eusebius, 6.25.1-2.
[8]*Ibid.*, 6.25.8.
[9]*Ibid.*, 6.25.10.
[10]*Ibid.*, 6.25.14.
[11]Robert M. Grant, *The Formation of the New Testament* (New York: Harper & Row, 1965) 171ff..
[12]Eusebius, 7.25.1-27.
[13]Grant, 173.

Chapter Four

A Return to the West

At this juncture in our study of the canon of scriptures, two men from the churches of the West claim our special attention. One is Jerome, who, because of his ardent commitment to the study of scriptures, was urged by Bishop Damascus in A.D. 382 to undertake a revision of the Latin version of the New Testament. The other is Augustine, a contemporary of Jerome, who became a famous apologist and theologian for the Western Church.

Jerome was born in Stridon on the borders of Dalmatia in A.D. 345 and died in A.D. 420. As did some of the churchmen of the East he traveled widely and gained valuable information concerning the books of the Bible. Jerome studied in Rome in the school of Donatus and attained an exceptional skill in Greek and Latin literature. In his travels to the East he came to Antioch and, after a severe illness in that city in A.D. 373, made a decision to devote himself to the study of the scriptures. After spending five years in the desert learning Hebrew from a Jewish Christian and at the same time becoming familiar with the Aramaic vernacular in the areas where he stayed, he returned to Antioch and was ordained a presbyter. From Antioch he went to Constantinople to hear Gregory of Nazianzus and was in the city when the council convened in A.D. 381. After a stay of three years in Rome (A.D. 382–385), he returned to Antioch, then to Egypt, and finally to Bethlehem in Palestine where he spent the rest of his life (A.D. 386–420).

In his first installment of the revision of the Latin version of the New Testament (the Four Gospels) that he sent to Bishop Damascus in A.D. 383, Jerome attached a letter to the bishop that included the following:

> You compelled me to make a new work out of an old; after so many copies of the scriptures have been dispersed throughout the whole world. I am now to occupy the seat of a judge, as it were, and seeing

they disagree, to decide which of them accords with the truth of the Greek; a pious task, truly, yet a perilous presumption, to pass judgment on others and oneself be judged by all.

In his letter, Jerome anticipated a negative response to his work but consoled himself with the reflection that it was Bishop Damascus who commissioned him to make a revision.

Whether Jerome completed the Latin translation of the rest of the New Testament is debatable. When Bishop Damascus died in A.D. 384, Jerome thought that he would be named successor. His dreams were not fulfilled because Siricus was elected. Soon after this Jerome went back to the East and finally settled in Bethlehem.

In the revision of the Latin Old Testament he started out by using the *Septuagint* but then decided to use the Hebrew text. In order to do this he had to have a better knowledge of the Hebrew language. We know of three Jewish instructors who helped him to become competent in the language. When he began his study of the Hebrew Bible, he became acutely aware of the fact that the Jewish collection contained only twenty-four books and that the apocryphal books were missing. While he admitted that these books were not in the canon, he believed that they had ethical value. Most of the books of the Apocrypha he allowed to remain in their existing Latin version. He did translate *Tobit* and *Judith* from Aramaic and the book of *Esther* from Hebrew but kept the *additions to Esther* in the Old Latin. The revision of the Old and New Testaments of Jerome is known as the *Vulgate.* In the Council of Trent in 1546, the prelates declared the Vulgate to be the standardized Latin version, but it took fifty years to clear the Old Latin corruptions that had crept back into the text of Jerome.

Jerome declared firmly that canonicity was not based on apostolic authorship, nor was it essential to know the author of a particular document in order to include it in a sacred collection (*Epistle* 129.3). Heretofore, the apostolic standard and known authorship were matters of vital concern for the Church Fathers. Concerning the catholic epistles, all of which he accepted, he was aware of questions about four of them. He said of the book of James: "Some claim that it was published by another person under James' name and gradually gained authority as time went on."[1] Concerning 2 Peter he said: "On account of its stylistic differences from the first (i. e., 1 Peter), it is considered by many not to be by him."[2] The difference in style he believes was due to the use of two translators by Peter. He named John the apostle as the author of 1 John but ascribed 2 and 3 John to John the elder of the Papias tradition. As to Jude, Jerome ascribed the short epistle to "Jude, the brother of James," but noted that it is rejected by some because the author quoted from 1 Enoch.[3] Despite the opposition to the epistle, he affirmed its authenticity saying, "Nevertheless by age and use it has gained authority and is reckoned among the holy scriptures."[4]

Jerome gave testimony to the validity of Hebrews as a Pauline epistle in the churches of the East, but added that many were of the opinion that it was by Barnabas or Clement of Rome. He admitted that the Western churches did not receive the epistle among the canonical scriptures; contrariwise, the Greek churches did not accept the book of Revelation. "Yet," he said, "we accept them both" (*Epistle* 129.3). Strangely enough, Jerome showed by a most trivial circumstance that he looked upon the *Epistle of Barnabas* as being close to canonization. In A.D. 388 while in Bethlehem, he wrote *On Hebrew Names*, in which he listed the proper names in both Testaments, giving their meaning, book by book. Every book in the New Testament appeared in the list except 2 John, which does not contain a proper name. At the end of the New Testament he gave thirteen names from the *Epistle of Barnabas*. This indicates he almost or did canonize Barnabas. His high regard for the epistle may have been the result of the Alexandrian school's high estimation of the document.

Jerome was no penetrating critic; he merely repeated the critical evaluations of others. As a rule he was quarrelsome and obsessed with a sense of his own self-importance, but relative to the list of New Testament books he seems to have acquiesced peacefully in accepting the books used in the churches. His only detectable deviation from the tradition of the churches was in relegating the books of the Old Testament external to the Hebrew canon to a classification known as *The Apocrypha*.

Augustine

Augustine, a friend of Jerome, was born in Tagaste, Numidia (which is now East Algeria), in A.D. 353. His father, Patricius, was a pagan, but

Monica, his mother, was a very dedicated Christian. When he was sixteen years of age, his father sent him to study in Carthage for three years. There he was motivated in his love of truth by reading Cicero's work, *Hortensius*. In his *Confessions* Augustine tells us of his wild and sinful life during his youth and early manhood. He was fascinated by Manichaeism, and for ten years he was a member of that sect. Augustine was a very capable rhetorician and taught rhetoric in his hometown of Tagaste, in Carthage, and in Rome.

Symmachus, the prefect of Rome, learned of his outstanding ability and sent him to Milan to teach rhetoric. In Milan he heard Ambrose, the bishop of Milan, preach and was converted to Christianity. Augustine said it was only when he discovered the allegorical method of interpretation of the Old Testament through Ambrose that he was able to become a Christian. The reason that he had hesitated in becoming a Christian was because of the influence of the Manichees over his life. They interpreted the Old Testament literally and by this method discredited the patriarchs of the Old Testament.

Though Augustine was not on a par with Jerome as a scholar (he did not know Hebrew and knew only a little Greek), he did possess a keen insight into the meaning of the Scriptures. For some time he hesitated in the acceptance of Jerome's Latin version because he felt that classical Latin was stiff and unspiritual, whereas the Old Latin versions contained more Hebraic emotion and imagery.

Augustine, in his list of the canon of the Old Testament, included *Tobit, Judith, 1 and 2 Maccabees*, the *Wisdom of Solomon*, and *Jesus ben Sira*. Concerning *Jesus ben Sira* and the *Wisdom of Solomon*, he said that they were to be numbered among the prophets "since they have won recognition as being authoritative" (*On Christian Doctrine* 2.13). His catalogue of the New Testament books followed the listing of the Old Testament, and all twenty-seven books are included. Without hesitation, he designated Paul as the author of Hebrews, though in other places we detect a feeling of hesitancy on his part with respect to the epistle. In later works where he quoted Hebrews, he avoided saying that Paul wrote it. Apparently, Augustine was in accord with Jerome in affirming that canonicity was based on neither apostolic authorship or knowledge of the name of the author.

Augustine showed that he was cognizant of degrees of value among the canonical books by the following:

Now, in regard to the canonical scriptures, he must follow the judgment of the greater number of Catholic churches; and among these, of course, a high place must be given to such as have been thought worthy to be the seat of an apostle and to receive epistles. Accordingly, among the canonical scriptures he will judge according to the following standard: to prefer those that are received by all the Catholic churches to those which some do not receive. Among those, again, which are not received by all, he will prefer such as have the sanction of the greater number (of churches) and those (churches) of greater authority, to such as are held by the smaller number (of churches) and those (churches) of less authority. If, however, he shall find that some books are held by a greater number of churches and others by churches of greater authority (though this is not a very likely thing to happen), I think that in such a case the authority on the two sides is to be looked upon as equal.[5]

Caspar Gregory said that the "important churches in Augustine's eyes are those that have apostolic bishops' seats: Alexandria, Antioch, Rome, and those that received epistles from apostles."[6]

Between A.D. 390 and A.D. 419, six councils were held in North Africa, four of which were in Carthage. The Council of Hippo in A.D. 393 set the limits of the canonical books. Augustine was still a presbyter at the time but very influential in the assembly. At the wish of the bishops he delivered before the council his discourse *De Fide et symbolo*. The complete acts of the council are lost; only through the Third Council of Carthage in A.D. 397 can we learn of the actions of Hippo. At this meeting an abridgment of the canons of Hippo was read and adopted. Among the canons adopted by the churchmen was a list of books of the Old Testament and New Testament. This was the catalogue previously given by Augustine, and he (now bishop of Hippo) was no doubt the ringleader in the formation of the canon on scripture. The decision on the books of the Bible was followed with this remarkable clause:

Let this be made known also to our brother and fellow presbyter Boniface, or to other bishops of those parts, for the purpose of confirming that Canon, because we have received from our fathers that those books must be read in the Church. Let it also be allowed that the Passions of the martyrs be read when their festival is kept.

Strangely, Boniface was mentioned, although he did not become pope until the death of Siricus in A.D. 418. This anachronism is generally explained by supposing that the canons of the six councils of North Africa were collected and codified after the confirmation of Boniface as Pope. Notably, the Third Council of Carthage was the first time that any assembly of bishops and presbyters made a proclamation about the limits of the scriptures. Heretofore, we have had opinions of individuals from the West and East. We should also bear in mind that the authority for closing the canon did not come from Rome but from North Africa.

In orthodox circles in the Western Church, the scholarly achievements of Jerome and the authoritative opinions of Augustine removed the lingering doubts about some books of the Bible. Just as churches in the East did not accept the list of Athanasius in his Festal Epistle of A.D. 367, so few churches in the West still accepted books that did not belong to the New Testament. Evidence for including other books in the New Testament comes from Codex Claromontanus, a bilingual (Latin and Greek) manuscript containing the epistles of Paul and Hebrews and dated in the sixth century. Between Philemon and Hebrews the scribe inserted a list of books including the *Epistle of Barnabas*, the *Shepherd of Hermas*, the *Acts of Paul*, and the *Revelation of Peter*. By accident he left out Philippians, 1 and 2 Thessalonians, and Hebrews. The manuscript represents a Western text and its origin is probably from a Western church. Even after the Western Goths became reconciled to the church in Rome, they continued to show their disdain for Revelation. As a result of their reaction the Council of Toledo in A.D. 633 declared that the ancient councils had validated the book as written by John the apostle. The decree of the council stated, "If anyone henceforth either shall not have accepted it (Revelation), or shall not have preached from it from Easter to Whitsuntide at the same time of mass in the church, he shall have the sentence of excommunication."

Two momentous events of the fifteenth century led to the revival of learning and ultimately to the Reformation in Europe. In 1453 Constantinople fell into the hands of the Muslims. The Christian and pagan scholars fled the city with their manuscripts and their Byzantine culture and came to Europe. Again the combined powers of the East and West met face to face. For some time the scholars of the East had gone their separate ways and did not maintain contact with the West. With their Greek manuscripts in hand they introduced a revival of learning in Europe. Greek art, science, architecture, and literature burst forth like a bolt of lightning from the blue. The second event was the invention of printing in 1454 by Johann Gutenberg of Mainz in the Rhineland. Formerly, individual copies of works had to be transcribed by hand, a time-consuming task and one subject to many errors. With the printing press, thousands of identical copies could be published at once.

The study of Greek made great inroads to the traditions of the Roman Catholic Church. The authority of usage of documents in the Roman tradition was being questioned, and the doors of criticism were unlocked. Erasmus, the leader of the literary and critical schools of the Reformation, published a Greek New Testament in 1516 and dedicated it to Pope Leo X. He called attention to the doubts that had been raised about certain books in the New Testament. He maintained that Hebrews was not written by Paul, though he went on to say that the reader should not consider it to be of less value; it was worthy of being read, regardless of whoever wrote it. In his commentary on James he accepted the epistle as authoritative but did not believe the writing as a whole presented "the dignity and gravity which we look for in an Apostle." Erasmus recalled the doubts concerning 2 Peter and Jude and assigned 2 and 3 John to John the Elder. On the book of Revelation he gave a rather lengthy discussion that seems to be a rehashing of the critical inquiry of Dionysius, bishop of Alexandria in the third century. He did not believe that John the apostle wrote it. Not only did he renew doubts as to the authorship of Revelation, but he insinuated that it had less value than other documents when he said that ancient theologians "quote passages from this book rather for illustration and ornament than for support of a serious proposition." The frankness of Erasmus in dealing with the New Testament was resented by the church, and in later years he became more reserved in his opinions. However, views similar to his were expressed by other Roman Catholics such as Cardinal Cajetan and Sixtus Senensis.

The most outspoken person of the Reformation on matters connected with the canon of scripture was Martin Luther. His judgments on the New Testament canon gained widespread recognition with his German translation in 1522 of Erasmus' 1519 edition of the Greek New Testament. In the preface to his first edition, he gave a general summary of the principles of the Christian life and concluded with his opinions of the documents. He gave priority to John's Gospel, 1 John, Romans, Galatians, Ephesians, and 1 Peter by saying, "These are the books which shew thee Christ and teach all which it is needful and blessed for thee to know, even if you never see or hear any other book, or any other doctrine." He believed that Hebrews was written by a disciple of the apostles—possibly Apollos—and not an apostle. While he admired the epistle of James, compared to his priority list, it was a "right strawy epistle" because it did not "preach and urge Christ." The right touchstone for Luther whereby all books of the Bible were to be criticized was whether they testify of Christ. If they did not teach Christ, they were not apostolic, even if they were written by Peter or Paul. On the other hand, he affirmed that whatever preaches Christ was apostolic—even if Judas, Annas, Pilate, and Herod preached it.

As for Jude, Luther said that it was an extract or copy from 2 Peter. Though he applauded it, he did not give to the book the same value as others. Current scholars would argue with Luther about Jude, for they would say that 2 Peter is an expansion of the ideas in Jude. Luther did not have much use for Revelation. In 1522 he said that it was neither apostolic nor prophetic, but in 1534—while he still considered it a dumb prophecy—he left it to the individual as to whether it was a work of John the Apostle. He admitted that the book could be used by Christians for consolation and warning.

In the table of contents of his 1522 German translation, Luther gave numbers to the list of New Testament books. There are twenty-three numbers followed by a space and then Hebrews, James, Jude, and Revelation without any serial numbers. This does not indicate that Luther put these four books out of the canon, but merely shows that these books were of lesser value for him. Like Jerome he made a distinction between the Hebrew canon of the Old Testament and the Apocrypha, but unlike Jerome—who allowed the Apocrypha to remain in his Old Testament Vulgate—Luther gathered the books of the Apocrypha and placed them in an appendix to the Old Testament in his German translation. He had little regard for the Apocrypha, especially *2 Maccabees*. His hatred for *2 Maccabees* was equal to his dislike for Esther.

Luther was, so far as we know, the first person to introduce the idea of a canon within the canon. This might have been hinted by Dionysius of Alexandria in his discussion of Revelation, but he hesitated to voice it openly. Oddly enough, when Luther was arguing with the Roman Catholics, he could say boldly that the Bible had absolute authority in every word written. When he spoke and wrote to those of his own communion, however, he maintained that there was a canon within the canon. The Gospel of John, the Psalms, Paul's epistles, 1 Peter, and 1 John ranked high on his list because they taught Christ plainly. Thus, on the one hand he could view scripture as absolute authority, and on the other hand he found its authority relative.

Among the friends of Luther was Andrew Bodenstein, generally known as Karlstadt (a name taken from his place of origin). As the Reformation advanced, Luther and Karlstadt became alienated from each other because of theological differences. While Karlstadt was still working with Luther he published a treatise, *On the Canonical Scripture.* The treatise was divided into five parts, but our interest is only in the fifth part, which presents a general classification of scripture. The first class contains the Pentateuch and the four Gospels. The second class includes the Prophets and the acknowledged epistles of the New Testament (thirteen of Paul, one of Peter, and one of John). The third group has the Writings of the Hebrew Canon and the seven disputed books of the New Testament (Hebrews, 2 Peter, James, Jude, 2 and 3 John, and Revelation). Acts is omitted probably because Karlstadt considered it a second volume of Luke. This treatise or the one entitled *What Books Are Biblical?* likely did not have a great influence on his contemporaries.

From Germany we look toward Switzerland to see what John Calvin, the Reformer of Geneva, said about the canon of the New Testament. Calvin wrote a commentary on every book of the New Testament except 2 and 3 John and Revelation. He occasionally quoted from Revelation, but these citations say nothing about his view of the book. It would be interesting to know why he did not comment on this work that had been disputed in the East. Calvin quoted from Eusebius frequently, so that we know he was acquainted with his vacillation concerning the document. Calvin recognized the value of Hebrews, but denied its Pauline authorship. He suggested that Luke or Clement of Rome might have been the author. He admitted that the epistle of James was not formerly received without a struggle. He embraced the epistle because there was "no sufficiently good reason for rejecting it." After declaring that there had been conflicting opinions about the epistle of Jude among the ancients, he went on to say that "because it is useful for reading, and does not contain anything foreign to the purity of Apostolic doctrine," he was willing to add it to the others. Calvin believed that 2 Peter was not written by Peter but by one of his disciples at Peter's command. He could not bring himself to the point of rejecting it "since the majesty of the Spirit of Christ exhibits itself in every part of the Epistle."

Calvin believed that the Bible was the very word of God guaranteed by the witness of the Holy Spirit, yet at the same time he could say that faith was not produced by every part of scripture. His argument of the witness of the Spirit is misleading. The Spirit did not protect a perfect text. In fact, the text of the Greek New Testament that he used is much inferior to the text that we now have from modern textual criticism. Certainly the Spirit did not lead the translators to give a perfect translation. Calvin also emphasized the power of the Spirit attending the preaching of the Word, but one cannot help wonder if he had ever heard a faultless sermon.

One might suppose that the Reformers would have retained a free position on the books of the Bible, especially since they raised questions about certain books. Luther willingly gave priority to certain writings and set forth a canon within the canon; so did Karlstadt and Erasmus. Calvin believed that the ritual laws in the Old Testament were irrelevant for Christianity, and he—contrary to the apostolic standard—courageously accepted the disputed catholic epistles and Hebrews. However, the Reformers failed to take an opportunity to make some changes and acquiesced to the tradition of the Roman Catholic Church. To be sure, they were not pressured by the authority of the church to accept the books of the Bible. Their acceptance of the writings was largely based on the subjective notion that the Holy Spirit's witness within them testified to the validity of the Bible.

As a result of the Reformers appealing to the Greek text for the New Testament and the Hebrew text for the Old Testament, plus their reaction to the Apocrypha, the Roman Catholic Church convened the Council of Trent in 1545 to clarify its own judgment as to the text and books of the Bible. In its third session beginning 4 February 1546, the subject of holy scripture and tradition was introduced for preliminary discussion. Four articles from the writings of Luther were set forth for consideration. The first article was the declaration by Luther that scripture alone (without tradition) was the only and complete source of doctrine. The second article had to do with Luther's belief that the Hebrew canon of the Old Testament and the acknowledged books of the New Testament should be accepted as authoritative. On the first point there was general agreement. The prelates concluded, in opposition to Luther, that tradition was coordinate with scripture and was a valid source of doctrine. With respect to the second matter there were four different opinions. On 15 March 1546, the council narrowed the views to one, and this judgment was passed by a majority of votes. The decree stemming from 15 March was finally published 8 April 1546.

For the first time in the history of the church the question of the contents of the Bible was settled and became an absolute article of faith carrying with it an anathema. The books of the Old Testament included, contrary to Jerome, the Apocrypha and the New Testament list of the twenty-seven books that we now have. In the 1546 decree the statement was made that only the *Vulgate* of Jerome was to be read in the churches. Of the fifty-three prelates present at the council, not one scholar was noted for his historical learning.

Notes

[1] Jerome, *On Illustrious Men*, 2.
[2] *Ibid.*, 1.
[3] *Ibid.*, 4.
[4] *Ibid.*, 4.
[5] Augustine, *On Christian Doctrine*, 2.12.
[6] Caspar Gregory, *Canon and Text of the New Testament* (Edinburgh: T & T Clark, 1907) 288.

Chapter Five

Criteria for the Selection of the Books of the Bible

Throughout this study the reader's attention has been directed to the external standards employed by the Jews for the formation of the Hebrew canon and by the early Christian church in canonizing the New Testament. It is now altogether fitting for us to review these criteria in order to ascertain their validity for us.

One of the criteria proposed was the apostolic authorship of the New Testament documents, but this could not be upheld. Mark and Luke, who wrote gospels, were not apostles. Irenaeus and Tertullian, who affirmed this principle, did not esteem Paul as an apostle in the true sense. He was not one of the Twelve, only a follower of the apostles. They, by a devious method, were able to legitimize him. In their use of Acts, which seems to have hitherto been unknown, Tertullian and Irenaeus took advantage of Paul's trip to Jerusalem to show that he was subservient to the apostles in Jerusalem. Not only that, but they changed the text in Galatians 2:5 to make Paul bend to the will of apostolic authority. After they legitimized Paul, they were able to put Luke in the apostolic tradition by saying that he was a travel companion of Paul and gained his information from him.

Tertullian rejected the epistle to the Hebrews because tradition said that Barnabas was the author, yet Barnabas—in the broader meaning of the term—was just as much an apostle as Paul. In the Muratorian canon there seems to be no doubt that Peter composed the Revelation of Peter, yet some did not accept the book. The *alogi* and Gaius of Rome rejected the Gospel of John because they said that it was not written by John the apostle but by Cerinthus, the Gnostic heretic. James and Jude were not apostles, but here again the apostolic standard had to be widened to declare their near-apostolic status since they were members of Jesus' family. 1 Peter was attested to from the first half of the second century, but 2 Peter was a late comer. Various theories were advanced to associate it with Peter the apostle, but it seems to have claimed canonization because there was nothing in the epistle unworthy of Peter.

1 John, though anonymous like the Gospel of John, was considered to be apostolic since it was written by the apostle who wrote the Gospel. Dionysius of Alexandria, in his literary criticism of Revelation, while recognizing it to be a genuine prophetic book, refused to believe that it was written by John the apostle. We credit Jerome and Augustine with good judgment because they both affirmed that canonicity was not dependent on the apostolic standard nor the need to know the author of a particular book. The apostolic standard led eventually to the exclusion of the *Shepherd of Hermas* and *1 Clement*, yet it was the authority of Clement of Rome based on apostolic succession that initiated the apostolic standard.

A second criterion for selection of the books of the Bible had to do with a time frame. Perhaps the Church Fathers established this principle for the New Testament, just as Josephus did for the Hebrew canon. Josephus defined the limits of the writings of the Old Testament within a period from Moses to the reign of Artaxerxes, because from the time of Artaxerxes there had been no succession of prophets. The ecclesiastical leaders carried over the same principle and related it to the apostles. Thus they fixed the time limit for a document to be a part of a second body of sacred literature within the apostolic age.

Our first confrontation with the criterion of antiquity is in the Muratorian canon. The author of the writing had a high regard for the *Shepherd of Hermas*. He was convinced that it was a genuine prophetic document, but it was too late to be considered among the prophets of the Old Testament and the apostolic writings. On the principle of antiquity we ask the question, "How ancient must a book be to gain acceptance?" The *Didache*, the *Letter of Clement of Rome to the Corinthians*, and the *Letters of Ignatius* of Antioch were written about the same time as, if not before, some of the writings in the New Testament. Indeed, this would have been a legitimate standard had they been competent enough to date the writings by appealing to evidence.

A third principle used to select the writings of the New Testament was universality. To be authoritative they must address the whole church. When Paul wrote his letters did he write to the whole church for all times? Certainly not. He wrote to individual churches beset with all sorts of problems—schisms, litigation against Christians, abnormal sexual practices, sacrificing meat to idols, divorce, remarriage, celibacy, following through on monetary pledges, conduct of women in worship, speaking in tongues, misunderstandings about the resurrection, behavior in the observance of the Lord's Supper, Judaizers, antinomians, ethical matters, family relationships, slavery, false views concerning the return of Christ, a defense of his apostleship, and many other issues—that, as spiritual director of the congregations, were incumbent on him to solve.

In our discussion of the Muratorian canon we have already drawn attention to the curious way that the author argued for the universality of Paul's epistles. How could such strained reasoning satisfy the minds of reasonable people? He began with Revelation, in which seven churches are addressed in letters that were meant for all. Then he returned to Paul, who wrote letters to seven churches, to show that he, too, wrote for all churches. Since seven is a complete number and John established the precedent for Paul, all the letters are universal in scope. The weakness of the argument is very evident. Paul wrote his letters before Revelation was written; therefore, he could not have followed the custom of John. Furthermore, Paul wrote to more than seven churches. When he wrote to the Galatians, more than one church was addressed.

Lest someone should bring up the letters that Paul wrote to individuals (Timothy, Titus, and Philemon) to refute his argument, the author of the Muratorian fragment would be quick to say, "They have been hallowed for the honor of the catholic church in the regulation of ecclesiastical discipline." Certainly the epistles of Paul have been helpful in our understanding of the Christian faith, but when Paul was writing he did not have future generations in mind.

A fourth criterion used by the church to accept writings was orthodoxy. This standard was less pronounced and remained more in the background, but it emerged in critical situations. By "correct teaching" the ecclesiastical officials meant the Christian truths that had been preserved in the undoubted apostolic documents and protected in the churches founded by apostles. With the rise of Gnosticism, Irenaeus appealed to the rule of faith or the rule of truth. The rule of faith was developed from the four Gospels and Paul's epistles, along with the oral tradition circulating in the churches of apostolic witness, and was the basis for what later was called the Apostle's Creed. Strangely enough, the rule of faith was used as a measure to validate orthodox literature, and concurrently the orthodox literature was employed to give validity to the rule of faith.

An excellent example of the criterion of orthodoxy is presented concerning the *Gospel of Peter*. Serapion, the bishop of Antioch, in A.D. 190 visited Rhossus, a village in his diocese. While he was there, he became aware of a disagreement over a Gospel ascribed to Peter. He settled the dispute by permitting the book to be read. He said, "As I had not read the Gospel which they put forth under the name of Peter, I said, 'If this is the only thing which occasions little of soul among you, let it be read.' " Since he supposed that all Christians in Rhossus held to the true faith, he considered the Gospel of Peter to be orthodox in nature. When Serapion returned to Antioch, he was able to get a copy of the Gospel from some docetists. After comparing the writing to other Gospels, he found elements of docetism in the *Gospel of Peter* and had it banished from the churches in his diocese. For reasons very similar to those of Serapion, the *alogi* rejected the Gospel of John. If orthodoxy had been the only principle used to admit writings into the canon, other early Christian documents would have found their way into the collection.

A fifth standard used by some Church Fathers was connected with usage in the churches. The appeal to traditional usage of writings is very conspicuous in Origen, Eusebius, and Augustine. Were the books customarily employed in worship and teaching in the churches? What was the tradition of the majority of churches? What if the usage of the majority of churches was in conflict with the books accepted by the churches with greater authority? These are some of the questions that were raised in the utilization of the writings.

Concerning 2 Peter, Eusebius said: "But the so-called second epistle [of Peter] we have not received as intestamented; nevertheless it has appeared useful to many, and has been studied with the other scriptures."[1] Thus, Eusebius showed that some hesitated to accept 2 Peter because it lacked broad recognition. The *Shepherd of Hermas*, *1 Clement*, the *Didache*, and the *Epistle of Barnabas* did not find their way into the canon, yet they had more support on the basis of church usage than did James, 2 Peter, 2 and 3 John.

A sixth criterion used by the ecclesiastical leaders, the principle of inspiration, has been supported by some. In the process of canonization of the Old Testament by the Jewish rabbis at Jamnia and the canonization of the New Testament by the Church Fathers, there was no claim for inspiration as a criterion until the time of Clement of Alexandria in the latter part of the second century or early part of the third century A.D. Yet Clement's criterion of inspiration permitted documents to be incorporated into the New Testament that no Christian would accept today. Clement allowed a wider range of books than was agreed to by other churches in the East and West, namely: the *Apocalypse of Peter*, *Preaching of Peter*, *Barnabas*, *1 Clement*, the *Didache*, and the *Shepherd of Hermas*. In the Muratorian Canon the author implied the principle of inspiration when he attempted to validate the epistles of Paul on the basis of the Revelation of John. The only writer of the New Testament who made a specific claim for prophetic inspiration was the author of the book of Revelation. The introduction to Revelation says, "The revelation of Jesus Christ, which God gave him to point out to his servants what things were bound to occur quickly, he made known to his servant John by sending his angel" (Rev 1:1). At the end of the book the author claimed that he was in the prophetic succession by his declaration that the document was a book of prophecy (22:9; 22:19).

No indication is given that inspiration of the Bible so greatly over-shadowed the process of canonization that the church leaders of Christendom considered the preservation of the books as providential.[2] After the books of the Bible were canonized, Christians through the ages have thought that the documents were included because they were inspired; this has led them to conclude that any book in the Bible is inspired because it is in the canon. By being misled by this presupposition, many Christians can argue for equal value of the books in the collection.

The criteria employed by the Church Fathers in determining the validity of a given book were often "insufficient and frequently wrong"[3] when viewed in the light of modern historical criticism. We do not offer any external standards as substitutes for the ones proposed in the past. Perhaps none are available for us at this time. Then, too, it would be impossible to take away or add to the formal canon of the Old and New Testaments that has been authoritative for Christians for centuries. It is not likely that any Christian would boldly declare that certain books should be excised from the Bible. However, in a covert manner a large majority do just that. They might not coin the expression of Luther that there is a "canon within the canon," but they do select those books and sometimes portions of books that meet their needs or that have more devotional value for them. The books which I choose may not correspond to those that my neighbor prefers.

In my thirty years of teaching the canon of the Bible at both the undergraduate and graduate levels, I have frequently asked the classes for a show of hands relative to the books of the Bible that they had read recently. Interestingly enough, the majority had read the Gospels, Acts, Paul's epistles, the Prophets, 1 John, and Deuteronomy. There seemed to be little concern for 1 Peter, 2 Peter, Hebrews, James, Jude, 2 and 3 John, Revelation, and the other books of the Old Testament. After polling the students I would say, "You have indicated by your selection that you have a canon within the canon." They would never commit themselves to declaring why this choice was made. Perhaps they made their choice because of the intrinsic value of the writings.

Martin Luther made a judgment on the basis of the internal worth of the scriptures. His touchstone by which he criticized books of the Bible was whether they preached or urged Christ. From the Old Testament he chose Psalms and from the New Testament he selected John's Gospel, 1 John, Paul's epistles (especially those to the Romans, Galatians, and Ephesians), and 1 Peter. Luther did not try to impose his own views on others in his preference. We heartily commend him for this, because what I might choose and what you might choose would be an altogether different list. Nevertheless, each Christian must have some internal principle for the evaluation of the intrinsic worth of the scriptures.

In this study of the canon of scripture it has been necessary to stress the problems connected with the selection of the books in the collection. I did not intend to disturb long-settled and cherished opinions, but I attempted to show the conditions that must be be considered in constructing a theory of scripture. If we take the historical review of the canon of the Bible seriously, inevitably old-fashioned opinions of the Bible will have to be revised. Let us not forget that the Bible itself is not the ultimate revelation and inspiration, but rather it is God to whom the Bible bears witness. The unique value of scripture is not found in its superiority over other literary artists and philosophers because of its predictions, its mine of wisdom, its poetry, or its insights about human nature, but because it is closely and inseparably joined with the revealing activity of God in human history.

Heretofore little has been said about inspiration, revelation, and the authority of the Bible. In the concluding chapter of this book I shall consider these topics because of their interrelatedness to the issue of how we got our Bible.

Notes

[1]Eusebius, 3.3.1.

[2]Krister Stendahl, "The Apocalypse of John and the Epistles of Paul in the Muratorian Fragment" in *Current Issues in New Testament Interpretation*, ed. W. Klassen and G. F. Snyder (New York: Harper & Row, 1962) 245.

[3]Kurt Aland, *The Problem of the New Testament Canon* (Oxford: A.R. Mowbray & Co., 1962) 14.

Chapter Six

Revelation, Inspiration, and Authority of the Bible

Inspiration is a vague term; it has no precise meaning. Does inspiration reveal anything or does it just motivate a person to do something that willpower is unable to accomplish? Some Protestants and Roman Catholics define distinctly what they mean by the word as it pertains to the Bible. They use the adjectives "verbal" or "plenary verbal" to qualify it, whether one or two adjectives are prefixed to "inspiration," the meaning is about the same. For them the entire body of scripture consists of words dictated by God in a sense unlike other writings with which we are acquainted. What the dictation indicates no one is able to say because we have no evidence that anyone has experienced "inspiration." To affirm that inspiration guarantees perfection is an unwarranted assumption and does disservice to God.

Indeed, I do believe in the inspiration of the authors of the books of the Bible as well as the authors of apocryphal writings. Though it is doubtful that a person could write anything unless there was some degree of inspiration, however, we must admit there is very little evidence that the Bible makes this claim for itself. One may refer to 2 Timothy 3:16 as a case in point. Here the writer is making a distinction between a writing that is "God-breathed" and other writings that do not have this qualification. Only "God-breathed" writing "is profitable also for teaching, for reproof, for correction, and instruction that is in the area of righteousness." The scripture to which the author of 2 Timothy refers is the Old Testament, and he intimates that some of this body of literature is not able to perform the function of the "God-breathed" part. 2 Peter

1:21 seems to eliminate the human element in prophecy, and from this statement one could surmise that inspiration involves dictation, but this opinion of 2 Peter stands alone.

When inspiration is described as verbal, we are pressed into the position of including other books in our canon. Certainly, the Roman Catholic Church accepts the Apocrypha. The early church frequently used the Apocrypha and other apocryphal writings. Much of the epistle of Jude is composed from the Assumption of Moses and 1 Enoch. In addition to actual quotations, there are many allusions in the New Testament to the *Wisdom of Solomon, Jesus ben Sira,* and to rabbinical midrashim.

Many sources that have been lost are referred to in the Old Testament, and the authors used those sources to compose their documents. In 1 and 2 Kings the authors mention the "Acts of Solomon" (1 Kgs 11:41), "The Chronicles of the Kings of Judah" (1 Kgs 14:29 and fourteen other places), and "The Chronicles of the Kings of Israel" (1 Kgs 14:19 and sixteen other places). Also, what are we to say about the "Book of the Wars of the Lord" (2 Sam 1:18) and the "Chronicles of Samuel, Nathan, and Gad" (1 Chron 29:29)? Did God dictate to Paul what Aratus said in his *Phaenomena* (Acts 17:28); or the quotation from Menander, the Attic poet (1 Cor 15:33); or the two statements from Epimenides, the Cretan poet (Acts 17:28; Titus 1:12)? Surely one would have to say that these documents were the inspired Word of God since they were used as sources by the authors of scripture. How can we hold to a dictation theory when writers were dependent upon other writers?

Unquestionably, I believe that the writers of the Bible wrote by means of the inspiration of God, but to say that the content of their messages was dictated by God has no validity and is pure speculation. Also, to say that the authors were inspired in no way suggests that what they wrote contained a greater degree of inspiration than that given to a teacher or minister of the gospel in our own day. The power of God's Spirit was not restricted to a few individuals in the past but is available to all who submit to God in the present. Inspiration was not just for those who wrote the books of the Bible but equally for those who determined the canon; transmitted, translated, and interpreted the text, as well as for those who preach, teach, and live the good news in Christ.

While a few Palestinian rabbis may have supported something akin to a dictation theory of inspiration of scripture, the vast majority did not. In Judaism the prominent spokesman for this theory was a contemporary of Jesus, Philo, a Jewish philosopher from Alexandria in Egypt. He taught that the scriptures came in a spasm of self-annihilating ecstasy. Philo believed that the sacred books were written in a condition of ecstasy that completely obliterated human powers. They were holy oracles that came by divine ventriloquism. For Philo the scriptures, as he read them in Greek not Hebrew, were oracular utterances with characteristics customarily attributed by the Greeks to Oracles. They were accepted as divine wisdom hidden under a system of curious riddles and symbols.

Philo arrived at this view of inspiration not by way of Hebrew thought but through his study of Plato and the Stoics. He was also influenced by his mystical experiences. He said that he was lifted out of an ordinary life of successive thoughts and feelings and entered an area where the flow of time ceased. His soul was absorbed into the eternal now, and he came into contact with God directly. Philo's mystical experience had an affinity with Plato's language in the *Symposium* and *Phaedrus* and not with the Old Testament concept of man's encounter with God. An experience like Philo's might be found in the scriptures in the vision of Isaiah, Ezekiel, and the Apostle Paul in 2 Corinthians 12, but these are incidental. The essence of Jewish religion is not found in mystical experience but in the conformity of the human will to God's will in practical everyday life (Mic 6:8 and Matt 7:21).

Strangely enough, the influence of Philo affected tremendously the Christian teachers in Alexandria for centuries. Clement and Origen accepted not only his allegorical method of interpretation but also his Greek concept of the scriptures as being oracular utterances. Philo's influence was not confined to Alexandria but was carried like the waves of the sea into all Christendom.

Too often we confuse inspiration with revelation. Especially is this true when we say that the Bible is verbally inspired. God revealed God's self to humanity through nature, by his mighty acts in history, as well as in the consciousness of individuals. The Bible is an account of this action of God and mankind's response to God's revelation whether it be a positive or a negative response. It is also a record of man's understanding of that revelation in accordance with his spiritual receptiveness.

The Bible tells us about a "life world"—not an abstract world or a thing world. In this library of sixty-six books we become spectators and participants in the drama of human history. We see a murdering Cain, a lying Abraham, a deceitful Jacob, a conniving David, a tyrannical

Solomon, a jealous Samuel and Saul, and disciples of Jesus struggling for power. We also see an Abraham who believed in God, a Moses who trusted God in the deliverance of the Israelites from Egyptian slavery, an Isaiah with a hope for the future, a Hosea who understood the love of God, an Amos who preached the justice of God, a suffering Job, Stephen (the first Christian martyr), and an undaunted Paul. More than these, we see God incarnate in Jesus Christ. Yes, this library deals with the human situation. There are stories of rape, murder, incest, trickery, war, religious persecution, church fights, heavenly visions, hymns of hope, and adventures in faith.

The Bible was written in different languages, different styles, and in different ages. Its authors were shepherds, farmers, warriors, poets, priests, historians, kings, a converted rabbi, Jewish Christians, Gentile Christians, sages, apostles, and scribes. While the authors of the Bible were from all walks of life and were fully aware of their human situation, they presented man's struggle against the backdrop of an encounter with God. The Bible is not merely a human book, nor can we say that it is a purely divine book. The divine and the human are intertwined.

By considering the human authors of the Bible as passive instruments in the hands of God, writing fully under divine control and producing a document for which God is totally responsible, the Bible becomes uniform in all levels of revelation. But is this really true? Just a cursory reading of the Old Testament reveals to the average reader a great contrast between the revelation of God's character and the New Testament presentation. Some are offended by the primitive barbaric images of God, subhuman ethics, and perverse nationalism. Without even listing the numerous discrepancies, doublets, and inaccurate statements in the Old Testament, which are inevitable as long as imperfect individuals write, one must consider a matter of more vital importance. This matter is the view of God's character presented in certain portions of the Old Testament. Did God command the Israelites to institute *cherem*, the absolute annihilation of their enemies and property with no exemptions—not even the old men, women, children, and babies? Against this perspective we have the final revelation of God in Jesus Christ who said, "Love your enemies and pray for those who persecute you" (Matt 5:44).

In the Old Testament the most shocking things are done in the name of God. What about a number of the Psalms that invoke curses upon the enemies of the people of Israel? Do these reflect the true character of

God? My Christian conscience will not permit me to read certain psalms before a congregation unless I delete in my reading the objectionable verses.

What we know of God in the Old Testament is valid if it is consistent with the revelation of God in Jesus Christ. The failure of Israel to comprehend clearly God's revealing activity, however, is not consistent with the revelation of God in Christ. We are forced to the conclusion that the witnesses to God's revelation in the Old Testament, no matter how much they were inspired, at times misrepresented the character of God.

Does this mean then that the Old Testament, which has an inferior revelation, is no longer of value to us? Should we discard the Old Testament as Marcion did in the second century A.D.? Not at all. Marcion was troubled because he saw a great contrast between the character of God revealed in Jesus Christ. In his day, biblical exegesis afforded him only one alternative to overcome this conflict. That alternative was the allegorical interpretation of the scriptures initiated by Philo. Marcion refused to accept this exit.

While the criterion by which we evaluate the Old Testament is the authority of Christ in the New Testament, it is essential for us to have the Old Testament so that we can understand the New. Not only should we use for this purpose the Old Testament but also the apocryphal writings, rabbinical literature, archaeology, and the data of history. Rather than stressing the contrast between the revelation of God in the Bible, we should look for the continuity. The God who revealed himself to Israel in the Old Testament also revealed himself completely in Jesus Christ of the New Testament. because humans could not fully comprehend the character of God in nature, in the events of history, and in human consciousness, God came to us in the flesh in Jesus Christ.

The authors of the Bible were real human beings who were fully responsible for their writings just as we are for ours. God did not reveal God's self through a book but through personality, and he did this perfectly in Jesus Christ, who was person and not book. In the Old Testament the revelation of God was obscured to some degree by the person through whom the consciousness of God came. However, in Christ the revelation was not obscured. Thus the revelation of God is dependent for its trustworthiness not just upon God, the source of revelation, but also upon the individual through whom this revelation comes. We are not to imagine that a person's selfhood was suspended when he was inspired to write about the revelation that he received from God. The author's message was always related to his own thought and outlook, and the form that he gave to it was his own casting. Therefore, as such, it was not a perfect Word of God even if it did have abiding significance. It is not that God progressively revealed himself, as some suppose, but that humanity progressively understood the givenness of God. This gradual understanding of God cannot be measured chronologically on an upward scale because in the history of Israel there are heights and depths of comprehension on the pilgrimage.

If we say that the Old Testament authors were inspired to write out of their experience of God's revelation that was not perceived in its fullness, does this mean that the New Testament writers, the disciples of Jesus, and the Jews in Palestine, who witnessed the revelation of God incarnate in Jesus, were also subject to a variety of opinions concerning his life, works, deeds, and mission in life? When Jesus taught in Galilee and Judea, the people did not respond in the same way. Some thought he was a political messiah, and they wanted to make him king. Many of the Pharisees considered him a threat to their authority as teachers. The Sadducees looked upon him as an insurrectionist who could destroy their position as keepers of the peace with Rome.

Jesus' own disciples misunderstood him to the very end. At Caesarea-Philippi Peter confessed that Jesus was the messiah. Immediately Jesus explained that he was to suffer and be killed. Peter reprimanded Jesus for entertaining the thought that the messiah should suffer. Clearly, Peter had his hope set on Jesus as a political messiah. Understanding the nature of the confession, Jesus reprimanded Peter before all of the disciples saying, "Get behind me Satan, you are not thinking the thoughts of God, but the thoughts of men" (Mark 8:33). The disciples disputed among themselves concerning who would be greatest in the political kingdom established by Jesus (Luke 22:24). They also failed to comprehend the teaching of some of the parables. Judas betrayed Jesus, and between the crucifixion and the resurrection the rest of the disciples were confident that the whole movement was terminated. Here was God in the flesh in the midst of his disciples and the religious leaders of Judaism, but selfishness, pride, and prejudice kept them from seeing the complete revelation of God.

Even the New Testament comes to us through personality that is subject to limitations. When the followers of Jesus experienced resurrection, they could confess Jesus as Lord, and by the word Lord they meant that he was equal to God of the Old Testament. They were witnesses of that event, and they proclaimed orally the meaning of that event for many years. The record of that revelation makes its way to us through people who were acquainted with traditions, oral and written, issuing from their own Christian community.

Only a small part of the primitive Christian discussion has been transmitted to us. This is very clear from John's Gospel when the author said, "Now Jesus did many other signs in the presence of the disciples, which are not written in this book, but these are written that you may believe that Jesus is the Christ, the Son of God, and that believing you may have life in his name" (20:30-31). Luke made the same affirmation in the preface to his Gospel. "Since many have undertaken to compile a narrative of the things which have been accomplished among us . . . it seemed good to me also . . . to write an orderly account for you" (1:1-3). The authors of the Gospels were selective in their materials and adapted them in accordance with their theological stance and their purpose in writing. Thus, when we read the Gospels, we relive only a minimum of what actually happened.

In the Synoptic Gospels we discover similarities and differences in the tradition. When we compare the Synoptics with John's Gospel, we see a vast amount of material not found in the Synoptics as well as material omitted. If there are variations in the Gospel accounts, shall we say that they are not reliable in giving us a revelation of the character of God in Christ even though there are variations? If all of the Gospels presented the same story without any differences, we would immediately suspect collusion. The witnesses are more trustworthy when the details of the story do not coincide perfectly. Now if the Gospels had come to us through dictation and the suppression of the personality of the authors, there would be no variations, and the account of the story would be suspect.

Most of the New Testament writers looked for a catastrophic end of history and the establishment of a new order. As the years passed the expectation of the parousia, revelation, and epiphany of Christ did not occur. Many of the Christians began to doubt the validity of the hope. 2 Peter was a last stand for that expectation; the author affirmed that the delay was due to the patience of God, who wanted all people to repent (3:3-9). This still does not excuse the misconception of Paul, however, who believed that this event would take place in his own lifetime (1 Cor

15:51f.; 1 Thess 4:15). On this basis, how can inspiration give us verbal infallibility?

Paul's letters constitute a large portion of the New Testament. One can hardly imagine his saying to his travel companions, "Today I feel inspired, so it is a good day to write scripture." Paul would be surprised to learn that what he wrote *was* scripture. He wrote letters to churches that either he or his friend Epaphras had established—as in the case of Colossae, Laodicea, and Hierapolis. He also wrote to the Christian community in Rome, giving his theological position in anticipation of visiting that fellowship. His letters were in the regular epistolary form of that day. All of the churches had problems of some sort, and, as spiritual director of those congregations, he rose to the occasion to give spiritual guidance in a time of crisis.

When the authors of the Bible have done the work they have been led to do, and they have introduced us to God whom they have experienced, it is not disastrous to our faith if we should evaluate the Bible book by book. But one might ask, "By what standard?" In the Christian faith we see the norm of truth about God in his revelation to us in Christ. By this norm we judge past, present, and future revelation. Are we irreverent if we challenge the logic of Paul? Certainly not. What he said about women in 1 Corinthians was essential for the Christians in Corinth where prostitution was rampant, but we are not to construe his teaching as binding on other churches where the problem did not exist or as restrictions being placed on women in our own day. Many of Paul's arguments are very flimsy in his epistles, but the thought patterns of his time demanded the use of rabbinical exegesis, the Stoic diatribe, and other forms. We applaud him for his use of the tools at hand.

The shortcomings of the prophets, the apostles, and other witnesses do not destroy the real religious testimony that they set forth on the whole. The revelation of God was disclosed through persons, and this disclosure is left to carry its own weight with those to whom the revelation is transmitted. If we trust in the Bible as the guarantee of faith, we have moved from faith and clamor for sight. Even the New Testament writers could not fathom the depth of God's meaning through the life, words, and deeds of Christ. The mystery of God is too great for us to comprehend in a book. If we could grasp the fullness of God's mystery, we would be God ourselves.

Those who opt for a static view of inspiration do so because they are afraid that any error in the Bible would destroy their faith. This fear is sheer nonsense. We do not hold contempt for secular literature if the writer gives historical inaccuracies, has discrepancies, or is inconsistent. Nor do we despise a minister of Christ who gets his facts of history jumbled up, misquotes a piece of literature, or even quotes a passage of scripture incorrectly. If the minister is inspired of God, his or her message can still warm out hearts and challenge us to a better Christian life.

Authority of the Bible

The question of the authority of the Bible is distinct from the question of inspiration and revelation, yet they are so intertwined that to separate them is impossible. There are no less than eight definitions of authority in the dictionary; thus, we have a problem of selection. What definition more accurately fits the picture of biblical authority? Are we to assume that the authority of the Bible is consonant with all meanings of the word? According to some, authority is the right or power to give commands and to enforce obedience. For others it is the reliability of a source, an expert, or a witness. Still others say that it is the self-assurance and expertness that comes with experience.

A large portion of knowledge that we accumulate comes by way of authority. A person who is a specialist in a given area evokes a response of dependableness from us. We believe that a person is reliable in his or her field, and we accept that one as an authority. Authority as a way of knowing, in essence, means that we are willing to accept what an alleged authority says is true, and we accept it precisely because the authority says that it is true. The authority should not protest if we desire to check out the findings for ourselves, provided there is the diligence or ability to do it. In our critical evaluation of the claims of the person, we ought to have the courtesy to accept those claims that are trustworthy. On the other hand, if we should discover ungrounded assertions of the authority, we can no longer believe in the authority for authority's sake. This does not mean that we reject the authority of the person completely, but we grant that status only in the areas of reliability.

In what sense can one say that the Bible has authority? Authority belongs to God, while the Bible derives its authority from God. Are the two equal? The only way that a person can equate God's authority with the scriptures is to say that God is the author: yet the Bible does not make that claim for itself. We have thrust this claim upon it. Those who say that God is the author of the scriptures usually mean that God is the one who dictated the message. The sole manner in which we can say God is the author of the Bible is to use the word author as meaning *originator*. Those books that were written came into existence by human hands. God's initiative and originating force gave the revelation to those who wrote, however imperfectly those writers might have comprehended that revelation.

According to Matthew 28:18 Jesus appeared to his disciples in Galilee after the resurrection and said, "All authority in heaven and on earth has been given to me." On the basis of his authority Jesus ordered his followers to make disciples, baptize them, and teach them all that he had taught. Jesus' authority was primary, but the witness to that authority was secondary.

The people of Galilee were amazed that Jesus' authority was superior to the scribes (Mark 1:22ff.). They were astonished because he had by-passed the system. The Pharisees had authority through ordination. According to their oral tradition, Moses laid his hands on Joshua; Joshua in turn laid his hands upon the elders; the elders laid their hands on the prophets; the prophets laid their hands on the men of the Great Synagogue; and the men of the Great Synagogue laid their hands on the rabbis. The Pharisees believed that when Moses placed his hands on Joshua, his personality entered Joshua and a rabbinic succession was established by ordination. This tradition comes from the Mishnah (*Pirke Aboth* 1:1). Rabbinic ordination (*semikha*) was initiated to transfer authority (*reshuth*) to the successive rabbis. This ordination could not be interrupted, or the authority would be broken. The surprise registered by the people in Mark 1:22 was based on Jesus' teaching and healing, the two gifts that came to rabbis through ordination. Yet they knew that Jesus had not been ordained as a rabbi. The people saw in him an authority that did not come through the regular channels. They recognized that Jesus' authority came directly from God and was not a derived authority.

In John's Gospel the author makes a similar claim for Jesus' authority. In the Prologue he states, "For the law was given through Moses; grace and truth occurred through Jesus Christ" (1:17). Moses received the law and transmitted it to the people; therefore Moses was a mediator between God and the people. In Christ we encounter no such mediation but experience the full revelation of divine intention and God's love for humanity. The Christ who reconciles us to God becomes his own authority for us.

C. H. Dodd recognized a difference between primary and secondary authority. Primary authority is *truth itself*, and secondary authority pertains to those who presume to know the truth as they *communicate* it to others. In Dodd's classification, God is primary authority while the Bible is a secondary authority. Thus the Bible is a report of those who have experienced God in history, in their own self-consciousness, and in nature. Others distinguish between absolute authority and educational authority. God is absolute authority. God has made God's self known in Jesus Christ. The Bible, as educational authority, is a witness to God's revelation for us. While both of these views are well-grounded, I am more inclined to agree with the view of Dodd.

The authority of God is manifested in three areas: the *Bible*, the *community of believers*, and the *individual*. All three of these are secondary and not primary authorities. They are authoritative when they mirror the primary and supreme authority. The harassing temptation of the Christian is to search for some secondary authority to use as a shield in warding off an encounter with God. The Pharisees had scripture, yet their sacred literature was used as a shelter to escape the revelation of God in Christ. They took refuge in their own interpretations of the law and built a fence around the intention of God. The Jews thought that they controlled the law when the oral tradition was codified and the Mishnah came into being. Then they interpreted the Mishnah and compiled the Babylonian and Palestinian Talmuds, thinking all the while that they had God boxed in. If we solely depend upon the report of what happened in history concerning God's dealing with people, ours becomes a second-hand religion. We must have a personal relationship with God to be a part of the community of believers in the pages of the Bible. Without this personal experience all else becomes just unintelligible chatter.

Millions of Christians will affirm that they accept the authority of the Bible from cover to cover, yet they have never read enough of it to come to any conclusion on their own. Their judgment is based entirely on what others have told them. They follow those who have shut God up in a book and accept an impersonal authority of a sacred document rather than the personal authority of a living God. The belief in infallible scripture and in an infallible church are efforts by Christians to make God's hidden sovereignty visible, tangible, and controllable to the extent that they displace the position that God alone occupies.

The Christ who is our authority comes to us through the experience of those who walked with him in his earthly ministry and witnessed the power of the resurrection by which he was declared Lord. The *kerygma* (proclamation) necessary for summoning people to believe in Christ as Lord and the *didache* (teaching) sufficient for understanding how the new life in Christ was to be lived could have been transmitted to us by word of mouth, as they were so ably delivered until the middle of the second century A.D. The possibility for inclusion of erroneous ideas certainly would have been much greater, however. Furthermore, there could have been no way to check the antecedent transmitters of the tradition.

If we should ask questions about the authority of the Bible, we are not questioning God's authority but the reliability of the authors who wrote the various books. Only in the sense that it is not incompatible with its human imperfections can we appropriately speak about an authority of the Bible; even then we are talking about a derived and secondary authority.

The authority of the Bible is enmeshed with an authority of selection of the thirty-nine books of the Old Testament and the twenty-seven books of the New Testament. My aim has been to deal with this authority in the present study of the canon. However, one cannot speak of the authority of the Bible without considering the authority of the text, translation, and interpretation. What is the correct text of the Old and New Testaments? Who has the correct and authoritative translation? What person or group of people can lay claim to the authoritative interpretation? Perhaps in a future book or books I will consider these matters, for whatever aids us in the understanding of the Bible helps us ultimately in our relationship with God through service, worship, prayer, and witness to his sovereignty revealed in Jesus Christ.

Glossary

Akiba—An influential rabbi of the first half of the second century A.D. Some believe that he collected oral traditions of the Jews and is responsible for the Tosefta.

Antiochus Epiphanes—One of the Seleucid line of kings who ruled over Syria from 175–164 B.C. In order to unify his empire he tried to uproot the religion of the Jews in Palestine. This action led to the Hasmonean revolt under Judas Maccabeas who finally regained religious freedom for the Jews in Palestine. Antiochus took the name Epiphanes, which means "manifest (God)." He claimed for himself deity.

Apocalyptic—A type of Jewish literature that propounded the view of a catastrophic intervention of God in history to overpower evil.

Apocrypha—A Greek neuter plural word that means "hidden" or "secret." It was first applied to literary works kept from the public because the doctrines were esoteric and had value only for the learned. Later, Apocrypha came to mean spurious or even heretical works. The technical term Apocrypha is applied to the non-canonical works of the Old and New Testaments. Numbered among the Old Testament Apocrypha are 1 and 2 Esdras, Tobit, Judith, Additions to Esther, Wisdom of Solomon, Jesus ben Sira, Baruch, Additions to Daniel, 1 and 2 Maccabees, and the Prayer of Manasseh. Roman Catholics accept all of these writings as deuterocanonical with the exception of 1 and 2 Esdras and the Prayer of Manasseh. The New Testament Apocrypha has spurious Gospels, Acts, Epistles, and Revelations.

Aratus—A Stoic poet who flourished in the middle of the third century B.C. He was from Soli in Cilicia.

Artaxerxes I—The son of Xerxes I and ruler over Persia from 464–424 B.C. During his reign Nehemiah returned to Jerusalem from exile to help in the construction of the wall around Jerusalem.

Babylonian Talmud—The word Talmud means "study." Talmud is a commentary on the Mishnah. In the third to sixth centuries A.D. the rabbis of Babylonia produced the Babylonian Talmud. This Talmud is far superior to the Jerusalem or Palestinian Talmud.

Clement of Rome—Bishop of Rome who wrote a letter to the church of Corinth about A.D. 90. He tried to use his influence to squelch a revolt against the leaders of the church. Some attribute a second letter to him that is more in the form of a homily.

Catholic epistles—Epistles in the New Testament that are more general in nature such as James; 1 and 2 Peter; 1, 2, and 3 John; and Jude.

Codex—A handwritten manuscript in book form.

Epimenides—A philosopher from the island of Crete who came to Athens about 500 B.C. He is quoted in Acts 17:28 and Titus 1:12.

Gaul—Modern France

Hegesippus—An ecclesiastical writer of the second century A.D. He probably flourished during the reigns of Antonius Pius and Marcus Aurelius.

Hillel—A native of Babylonia who came to Palestine to continue his studies under rabbis. He was known for his seven rules of interpretation and for establishing a school of rabbis in opposition to the more conservative rabbi Shammai. After the destruction of Jerusalem in A.D. 70 the principles of Shammai were no longer authoritative. The principles of the house of Hillel prevailed. Hillel died about A.D. 10.

Ignatius—Bishop of Antioch who was put to death under the reign of Trajan (A.D. 98–117). All that we know of him is through his seven letters (authentic ones) written to churches on his way to martyrdom in Rome.

Menander—An Attic poet who died about 300 B.C. Paul quotes this poet in 1 Corinthians 15:33.

Midrashim—A name given to the exegeses of the Bible by the rabbis in Palestine in the second century A.D.

Mishnah—The collection of the oral laws compiled by Judah ha-Nasi about A.D. 200. Some scholars believe that rabbi Akiba made the first collection, known as the Tosefta, some 70 years earlier.

Palestinian Talmud—A commentary on the Mishnah by the Palestinian rabbis. It was completed in the third century A.D. Some refer to this Talmud as the Jerusalem Talmud.

Ptolemy Philadelphus—One of the Hellenistic kings ruling in Egypt from 287–247 B.C. During his reign the Jews translated the Hebrew scriptures into Greek. This translation is known as the Septuagint.

Pseudepigrapha—A large group of Jewish writings outside the Old Testament canon and Apocrypha. These works include apocalypses, legendary history, psalms, and wisdom literature. This classification assumes that the whole collection consists of pseudonymous authors. This is not true, however. Many are not false writings appealing to a worthy person of the past as author. Some of the canonical Old Testament has pseudonymous writers such as Song of Songs, Daniel, and Ecclesiastes. This is also true of the Apocrypha with works like 1 and 2 Esdras, the Wisdom of Solomon, and the Prayer of Manasseh. Included in the Pseudepigrapha are such works as Testament of the Twelve Patriarchs, Jubilees, 1 Enoch, 2 Enoch, Assumption of Moses, the Martyrdom of Isaiah, and the Apocalypse of Baruch.

Qumran—The ruins of the Essene community that was the center for the Dead Sea Scrolls. It is on the west coast of the Dead Sea about eight miles south of Jericho.

Shammai—A very conservative rabbi who flourished the last half of the first century B.C. and the first part of the first century A.D. He organized a school of rabbinical thought in opposition to the more liberal rabbi Hillel.

Samaritans—The Hebrews who split with the Jews after the Jews returned from captivity under the Persians. Probably the split came when the habdalah movement of Ezra-Nehemiah became unbearable for the Hebrew people who had not gone into exile and constructed a separatist policy. The Samaritans preferred to call themselves Shomerim (keepers or guardians of the law). They did not believe in a Messiah but a tahev who was a prophet like Moses. This tahev would restore all things. The Samaritans like the Sadducees accepted only the first five books of the Old Testament.

Tanak—Frequently used by Jews to refer to their scriptures. Tanak is an acronym from the Hebrew Torah (Pentateuch), nebi'im (Prophets), and Kethubim (Writings).

Tannaim—Literally "teachers" (or "repeaters"), the rabbis of Palestine in the second century A.D. whose statements are contained primarily in the Mishnah.

Tosefta—A collection of oral laws that parallel the Mishnah. Some scholars believe that this work is before the Mishnah and was compiled by rabbi Akiba.

Uncial—The form of letters (large and rounded) that was characteristic of most Greek and Latin manuscripts between the fourth and ninth centuries A.D. After the ninth century the minuscule style was more common. The use of uncial is traced back to Jerome who used *uncialibus litteris*. The uncial is an inch high. To be sure the uncial manuscripts did not have inch-high letters. This is probably a hyperbole by Jerome.

Selected Bibliography

Aland, Kurt. *The Problem of the New Testament Canon.* Oxford: A. R. Mowbray and Co., 1962.

Barclay, William. *The Making of the Bible.* London: Lutterworth Press, 1965.

Barr, James. *Holy Scripture: Canon, Authority, Criticism.* Philadelphia: Westminster Press, 1983.

Bentzen, Aage. *Introduction of the Old Testament.* 2 vols.. Copenhagen: G.E.C. Gad Publisher, 1948.

Blackmon, E. C.. *Marcion and His Influence.* London: SPCK, 1948.

Bruce, F. F. *The Canon of Scripture.* Downers Grove IL: InterVarsity Press, 1988.

Chadwick, Henry. *The Early Church.* Grand Rapids MI: Harmondsworth, 1968.

Childs, B. S. *The New Testament as Cannon, An Introduction.* Philadelphia: Fortress Press, 1984.

Davies, J. G. *The Early Christian Church.* New York: Holt, Reinhart, & Winston, 1965.

Dodd, C. H. *The Bible Today.* Cambridge: University Press, 1947.

___ *The Authority of the Bible.* London: Fontana Press, 1960.

Ferris, G. H. *The Formation of the New Testament.* Philadelphia: Griffith & Rowland Press, 1907.

Gamble, Harry. *The New Testament Canon: Its Making and Meaning.* Philadelphia: Fortress Press, 1985.

Goppelt, Leonard. *Apostolic and Post-Apostolic Times.* New York: Harper and Row, 1970.

Grant, Robert M. *The Formation of the New Testament.* New York: Harper and Row, 1965.

___ *The Apostolic Fathers: A New Translation and Commentary.* 6 Vols. New York: Nelson, 1965.

Gregory, C. R. *Canon and Text of the New Testament.* Edinburgh: T & T Clark, 1907.

Harnack, Adolf. *The Origin of the New Testament*. New York: Macmillan Co., 1925.

Klassen, William and Graydon Snyder. eds. *Current Issues in New Testament Interpretation*. New York: Harper and Row, 1962.

Knox, John. *Marcion and the New Testament*. Chicago: University Press, 1942.

Metzger, Bruce. *The Canon of the New Testament*. Oxford: University Press, 1987.

Pfeiffer, Robert H. *Introduction to the Old Testament*. New York: Harper and Brothers, 1941.

Robinson, H. Wheeler. *Inspiration and Revelation of the Old Testament*. Oxford: Clarendan Press, 1946.

Rowley, H. H. *The Growth of the Old Testament*. London: Hutchinson and Co., 1950.

Ryle, H. E. *The Canon of the Old Testament*. Cambridge: University Press, 1904.

Sanders, J. A. *Torah and Canon*. Philadelphia: Fortress Press, 1972.

Souter, Alexander. *The Text and Canon of the New Testament*. New York: Scribner's Sons, 1913. Rev. ed. C. S. C. Williams. London: Duckworth, 1954.

Sparks, H. F. D. *The Formation of the New Testament*. London: SCM Press, 1952.

Westcott, B. F. *A General Survey of the History of the Canon of the New Testament*. Cambridge: University Press, 1889.